Make a Fortune
Promoting
Other People's
Stuff Online

Make a Fortune Promoting Other People's Stuff Online

How Affiliate Marketing Can Make You Rich

Rosalind Gardner

McGraw-Hill

New York   Chicago   San Francisco   Lisbon
London   Madrid   Mexico City   Milan   New Delhi
San Juan   Seoul   Singapore   Sydney   Toronto

1 2 3 4 5 6 7 8 9 0   DOC/DOC   0 9 8 7

ISBN-13: 978-0-07-147813-7
ISBN-10: 0-07-147813-2

This publication is designed to provide accurate and authoritative information in regard to the subject matter covered. It is sold with the understanding that the publisher is not engaged in rendering legal, accounting, or other professional service. If legal advice or other expert assistance is required, the services of a competent professional person should be sought.

> —*From a declaration of principles jointly adopted by a committee of the American Bar Association and a committee of publishers.*

McGraw-Hill books are available at special quantity discounts to use as premiums and sales promotions, or for use in corporate training programs. For more information, please write to the Director of Special Sales, Professional Publishing, McGraw-Hill, Two Penn Plaza, New York, NY 10121-2298. Or contact your local bookstore.

Library of Congress Cataloging-in-Publication Data

Gardner, Rosalind.
  Make a fortune promoting other people's stuff online : how affiliate marketing can make you rich / by Rosalind Gardner.
    p. cm.
  ISBN 0-07-147813-2 (pbk. : alk. paper)
  1. Internet marketing. 2. Multilevel marketing. 3. Business networks. I. Title.

HF5415.1265.G37 2007
658.8'72—dc22   2006103343

Contents

Acknowledgments

I am enormously grateful to the late Corey Rudl of the Internet Marketing Center. Corey profiled my affiliate business success story on his Secrets to Their Success site, and as a result I received hundreds of e-mails from aspiring netpreneurs who wanted to learn more about affiliate marketing on the Internet.

Their questions helped me realize that I had valuable information to share, and each and every question asked has provided another good reason to write *Make a Fortune Promoting Other People's Stuff Online: How Affiliate Marketing Can Make You Rich.*

I am therefore also grateful to everyone who ever asked me a question about doing business online as an affiliate marketer.

Last, but not least, I thank you, dear reader, for choosing to read this book. I hope it proves enormously beneficial to you in all your online moneymaking ventures!

With best wishes for your success,

—Rosalind Gardner

Introduction

Affiliate marketing, like many other online and offline businesses, is a dynamic, ever-evolving, time-consuming, sometimes frustrating and rewarding adventure. Like all businesses, it is about you and what resources you are willing to commit to have the life you want and meet your goals.

The true joy of becoming a super affiliate marketer is that affiliate marketing does not discriminate. Regardless of your ethnicity, age, religion, gender, or shoe size, you have the ability, with a little effort and a lot of determination, to walk away from your day job and focus on *your* business in *your* own environment.

From Joe, a 14-year-old with a penchant for heavy metal music, to Glenda, a stay-at-home mom with a Web site about children's party games, to Bill, a 70-year-old with a passion for growing organic pumpkins, you too can make it in this business if you follow the simple steps set out in this book.

HOW TO GET THE MOST FROM THIS BOOK

You are reading *Make a Fortune Promoting Other People's Stuff Online: How Affiliate Marketing Can Make You Rich* because you want to learn how to make money with affiliate programs, and you want to do that without reading an encyclopedia or spending a lot of money.

You will find this book a valuable resource that can help you reach your goals by teaching you what it takes to achieve them. You will find yourself returning to it time and time again as you follow the guidelines and build your own affiliate marketing business.

In order for you to get the most out of *Make a Fortune Promoting Other People's Stuff Online: How Affiliate Marketing Can Make You Rich* and increase your chances of becoming a successful affiliate marketer, please heed the following suggested action plan.

READ THE WHOLE BOOK

The prospect of having your own online business is very exciting, and you probably want to get started immediately. But remember to begin at the beginning and read this book in its entirety first. Highlight those sections of particular interest to you. Then use it as a mini-encyclopedia when you need to revisit a section you have previously read.

CONNECT TO THE INTERNET

Throughout the book you will find addresses for many recommended Web sites. URL's (uniform record locators, links, or Web site address) are noted in three different ways.

1. If the URL is long, or included within a paragraph, it is placed inside parentheses ( ) beside the Web site's name, as follows:

   Google Adsense (https://www.google.com/adsense/)

2. If the URL is placed on a separate line following a paragraph, the parentheses are eliminated, and written as follows:

   https://www.google.com/adsense/

3. Otherwise, the name and URL will be written as one word, for example,

    Tucows.com.

To visit the Web site mentioned, simply type the URL (without the parentheses) as you see it printed into your Web browser and click on "go."

Most browsers, such as Internet Explorer, Netscape, and Firefox, allow you to enter URLs without having to enter "http://" before the actual address, so you can simply type Tucows.com into the address bar, instead of http://tucows.com.

If you prefer to read *Make a Fortune Promoting Other People's Stuff Online: How Affiliate Marketing Can Make You Rich* all the way through first, that is okay too! Find a comfy sofa and your favorite beverage, and highlight those Web sites that you want to visit later. When you are finished reading, hop online and explore your list of Web site URLs.

TO SUCCEED, TAKE ACTION

A goal without a deadline is nothing more than a dream. To achieve success, you must set specific goals with target completion dates, and develop a plan to meet those goals. Read the book completely, and then act on your plan immediately! By approaching your work in bite-sized chunks, you will find that your project becomes easily manageable.

ALWAYS KEEP LEARNING

Internet technology, e-commerce, and affiliate marketing are all evolving daily. To stay current, affiliate and Internet marketers stay abreast of current trends by reading relevant newsletters, keeping an eye on their competitors, and investing in educational materials. I invite you to sign up for the *Net Profits Today (NPT)* free newsletter to stay current on Internet and affiliate marketing changes and developments. It is available at NetProfitsToday.com.

When you have finished reading *Make a Fortune Promoting Other People's Stuff Online: How Affiliate Marketing Can Make You Rich*, you will have all the information you need to start your own profitable affiliate marketing business quickly, easily, and inexpensively.

1

Start with the Basics

Affiliate marketing on the Internet isn't rocket science. You do not need an MBA or other degree to succeed. If you know how to surf the Internet, as well as send and receive e-mail, you have already mastered the two activities you will perform most often. Do not worry about having to learn HTML (hypertext markup language—the code used to write Web pages) right away. At this point we are dealing with only those things that will help you set up your office and maneuver around your computer more easily. Building a Web site comes later.

BASIC TOOLS, KNOWLEDGE, AND SOFTWARE

To start a part- or full-time business on the Internet, you will need some very basic equipment, or *hardware*, as well as services that allow you to connect to the Internet.

Dedicate One Computer to Your Business

Having a computer dedicated solely to your business is truly a *must*. Access to your business computer should be strictly limited. Kids, and even some adults, can inflict damage and cost your business significant amounts of time and money when infected software programs are downloaded.

Get the Fastest Internet Connection

Internet connection options in your area may include telephone, cable modem, or DSL. Telephone modems are slow, and the slower your Internet connection, the slower you are able to work. It takes longer to download your e-mail and longer to upload pages to your site. In addition, slow connections will cost you money in the long run. (If possible, avoid the telephone modem and sign up for a cable or DSL connection if it is available in your area.)

Example: Sam toils on his Web business with a slow-as-molasses 36.6K modem. He works about eight hours a day, six days a week, and uses that connection for about 50 percent of his work or 24 hours per week. Bob uses a cable connection that is about five times faster than Sam's telephone connection. Bob can therefore

---

SUPER AFFILIATE TIP

Basic computer skills, including a grasp of a few macros and file management techniques, will save you time in the long run.

Figure 1.1 Basic Macros

Keystrokes	Function
Ctrl-A	Select all
Ctrl-B	Bold
Ctrl-C	Copy
Ctrl-D	Bookmark
Ctrl-E	Center
Ctrl-F	Find
Ctrl-G	Go to
Ctrl-H	Replace
Ctrl-I	Italicize
Ctrl-J	Full justify
Ctrl-K	Hyperlink
Ctrl-M	Increase indent
Ctrl-N	New document
Ctrl-O	Open document
Ctrl-P	Print
Ctrl-R	Right justify
Ctrl-S	Save
Ctrl-T	Tab
Ctrl-U	Underline
Ctrl-V	Paste
Ctrl-W	Close document
Ctrl-X	Cut
Ctrl-Y	Redo/repeat last action
Ctrl-Z	Undo

accomplish in 12 minutes what it takes Sam an hour to do. In other words, to accomplish the same amount of work, Bob works only 4.8 hours to Sam's 24 hours—19.2 hours *less*.

In financial terms, it takes Sam five hours to earn what Bob earns in an hour, relative to their use of the Internet for uploading, downloading, and research. This calculation is a good example of what it means to be "penny wise and pound foolish." Get the fastest Internet connection available, and do not let $20 or $40 per month limit your earnings potential.

Work Faster with Macros

A *macro* is a way to automate a task that you perform repeatedly or handle on a regular basis. The macros (or computer codes) shown in Figure 1.1 are common across most Windows platforms. They are definitely worth memorizing insofar as the time they can save you while you're performing your daily tasks.

Organize Your Affiliate Data

Whether you have one site with five affiliate programs or ten sites and fifty affiliations, you need to keep track of your affiliate information and make it easily accessible while you work. To save time (and to keep your sanity), stay organized by establishing categories and file folders within your e-mail program with bookmarks and file folders containing all documents relevant to your Web business. Following are some suggestions for business categories:

- Accounting
- Advertising and marketing
- Codes and passwords

- Correspondence
- Financial
- Joint ventures
- Merchant partners
- My Web sites
- Newsletters
- Software

Store all your Web site files in folders named for their domains. All files belonging to those domains can then be stored in their appropriate folder. For example, if your site name is GirlieGoodies. com, create a file folder named "GirliesGoodies.com" (without the quotes) in the "My Documents" folder on your computer. Next, create folders within that folder for all the information related to that site. I recommend that you create one folder named "Admin" or "Administration" to hold site and affiliate program information.

Track Your Affiliate Data

Keeping track of programs joined through *affiliate networks* is easy because you will have only one username and password to remember. Once you are logged into a network's affiliate interface, you can access statistics and get banners and ad copy for all the merchants associated with that network. However, you will be provided with individual usernames and passwords for many of the independent programs that you join. If you have a good memory, you may be able to memorize all your important data, but most of us need help to keep track of everything.

Use a spreadsheet as you research, plan, and build your first site to list keywords, competitors, and the affiliate programs you join.

SUPER AFFILIATE TIP

Keep your data organized by using a spreadsheet like Excel. Input and organize your data in a way that makes sense to you. A spreadsheet is basically a computerized ledger, and presents the best way to keep track of many aspects of your Internet business. If you are new to Excel, I recommend Richard Kraneis's e-book, *The World's Shortest Excel Book* at http://www.TheWorldsShortestExcelBook.com.

Add a column, delete a column, or widen and narrow the columns. Add as many parameters as you like. Make the fonts any size and color that you see fit. Link your affiliate information spreadsheet to your conversion rate information spreadsheet and access either with a single click.

Here is a list of items that you may want to include on your affiliate information spreadsheet:

1. Program or company name
2. Your login or username
3. Password
4. Affiliate links
5. Affiliate program contact information
6. Commission information
7. Additional remarks about the program

Figure 1.2 is an example of a partial spreadsheet that lists affiliate data.

Figure 1.2   Partial Spreadsheet with Affiliate Data

Program name	Username	Password	Affiliate link
Article Announcer	Meme123	Sl9s388	http://wetrack.it/...
Article Automator	Meme123	greentee3	http://www.1shop...
Aweber	Meme123	pass3xx	http://www. aweber...

Keep a link to this spreadsheet on your computer's desktop so that it is easily accessible.

If Excel isn't installed on your computer, you may want to look into EasyOffice 5.1, which is available as freeware through Tucows, which gives it a "5 cow" rating. To find EasyOffice 5.1 and other similar programs, search for 'spreadsheet' at Tucows [http://tucows.com].

Remember to enter new data as soon as possible. The first time you forget to make a few entries and then spend five minutes searching your e-mail program for the information, or have to e-mail the company concerned to resend your codes, entering data immediately will start to become a habit.

Affiliate Organizer (http://OrganizedAffiliate.com) is specialized software for affiliates that lets you to store all your most important data from your day-to-day business. Here is a list of the information related to affiliate marketing that you can input into Affiliate Organizer:

• Adsense
• Advertising

- Autoresponder
- Blogs
- Contacts
- Domain registrars
- Forums
- Hosting
- Keyword lists
- Link partners
- Memberships
- Merchants
- Outsourced work
- Projects and ideas
- Resources
- Services
- Software
- Tasks/alerts
- Web sites
- Year plan

For example, in the Web sites section, you may store and later view information about each of your Web sites and its associated Web host, FTP address, user and passwords, start and end date, industry, merchants you have added, pay-per-click advertising campaigns currently running, reciprocal links, support e-mail, and phone numbers. Likewise, in the outsourced work section, you would input information about projects for which you have hired outside help, such as a Web site developer or graphic designer.

SUPER AFFILIATE TIP

Choose either a spreadsheet or Affiliate Organizer to keep track of your affiliate business information. Use it diligently to make your work faster and simpler.

This software is extremely easy to install. An icon appears in the system tray located in the bottom right-hand corner of your desktop, which makes the program simple to access. The program is also simple to use. Just fill in the blanks and hit "save." (Your data can also be backed up and restored at the click of a button, which is a huge relief for anyone who has ever lost data.)

Use Text Editors for Making Quick Notes

A text editor is a piece of computer software for editing plain text. Text editors do not have all the features of more robust word processing software, but they are extremely handy for making quick notes. Using a text editor will also eliminate many of the formatting characters that are embedded by more sophisticated word processing programs, such as Microsoft Word. These formatting characters may cause havoc with the appearance of Web pages and e-mail messages, so using a simple text editor eliminates the worry about text that is unnecessary.

Depending on the type of site-building software you use, you will create most of the content for your Web pages in a text editor before you upload them to your Web site. (It is also an excellent way to learn HTML.) NotePad is an easy-to-use text editor and is probably already installed on your computer if you are running Windows. UltraEdit Pro is another text editor and is available at Ultraedit.com.

Download File Extraction Software

If you have ever downloaded software or a large e-book from the Internet, you have probably downloaded a zip file. *Zip files* are files that are compressed to take up less space and bandwidth. Zip software or an *extraction utility* is used to extract zipped files. Following are two commonly used file extraction software packages:

- *WinZip* (for Windows users) is one of the most popular extraction utilities. WinZip compresses and decompresses files using the zip format. This is the most common format used on the Internet for compressing Windows files. Files compressed in this way are identified with the extension ~.zip. WinZip can be downloaded free from Tucows.com, Shareware.com, and Download.com.
- *Stuffit Expander* (for Mac users) is a utility that decodes and extracts Macintosh files downloaded from the Internet. Unlike Windows downloads, which must be decompressed, Macintosh downloads must be decompressed and decoded before they can be used. Fortunately, Stuffit Expander combines both these steps. Stuffit Expander can be downloaded at http://www.stuffit.com/expander/index.html.

Use the Google Toolbar to Surf and Research

To make Web surfing and market research easier and faster, download and install the free Google toolbar from http://toolbar.google. com. This toolbar allows you to search the Web from any browser

Figure 1.3 Google Toolbar

window or Web site without having to return to Google's homepage to start another search. The Google toolbar takes only a few seconds to install on your computer and is available in a variety of languages. Once installed, the Google toolbar appears in your Internet Explorer browser window, as displayed in Figure 1.3.

Handling Single, Recurring, and Optional Expenses

There are three types of business expenses you can expect as an affiliate marketer: one-time expenses, recurring expenses, and optional purchases. One-time expenses include:

- Computer
- Computer peripherals
- Office furniture
- Initial domain registration
- Software

Monthly, yearly, and irregular expenses include:

- Office supplies (such as pens, paper, printer ink, etc.).
- Advertising costs at pay-per-click search engines (advertising expenses vary depending on the budget you set and on the number of accounts you have set up).

- Web hosting (prices can range from as low as $3.95 per month for very small hosting packages with few features to more than $100 per month for a dedicated server that comes with all the bells and whistles and can handle the amount of traffic that generates millions of dollars in sales).
- Autoresponder services (a monthly fee of between $15 and $20 with additional charges when your mailing list grows beyond a set number of subscribers—usually for each additional 10,000 subscribers).
- Internet and telephone connections (set monthly fees that may increase when usage exceeds a specified amount).
- Domains need to be renewed yearly (or at whichever interval you selected during your initial registration).
- Business license (for which there may be an annual fee).

Optional purchases may include the following:

- As technologies and methods change and emerge rapidly on the Internet, continuing education and software enhancements will become an integral part of sustaining and growing your affiliate marketing business. Examples of ongoing education include courses, seminars, teleseminars, and industry conferences that you may choose to attend.
- Instead of learning to build your site from scratch, you might choose to hire a Web designer and ghostwriters to help build your site and content.
- There is plenty of software that can help make your business process faster and easier. Some examples include article distribution software like Article Announcer (http://www.articleannouncer.com) and Wordtracker (http://www.

wordtracker.com), a research tool that helps Internet marketers determine the potential profit of a niche based on existing supply and demand.

Your affiliate site can be simple and basic or full of the latest technological bells and whistles. Whichever end of the spectrum you decide to pursue is entirely up to you *and* what your budget will allow.

CREATE A POSITIVE WORK ENVIRONMENT

If you have a job outside your home, it is unlikely that you are able to control your work environment, but you certainly can enhance it if you have a home-based business. (Isn't that reason enough to strive to achieve a full-time affiliate business?)

Take a step back from your work space—whether it is a room set aside specifically for your office or a space you have created in the corner of the den. Use all your senses and notice the colors, sounds, smell, lighting, and view (if you are lucky enough to have one). What do you notice? Does your work space make you feel motivated and happy or uncomfortable and distracted? Is it set up efficiently so that everything you need is at hand, or is it disorganized and cluttered? Numerous scientific studies have shown that the colors you choose in your decor affect your mood. How do the colors around you make you feel? Calm and centered or nervous and edgy? Figure 1.4 contains a list of colors and what each represents.

Scientific studies have also shown that lighting can have an impact on the quality of your work. Good lighting in your workspace will improve your productivity and decrease fatigue and eyestrain, which in turn reduces errors.

Try to work in a space where you are facing a window, so the light is shining from behind your computer, not directly onto it. Take a break at least once every hour. Get up and stretch, walk around, and focus on something in the distance. Sitting at a computer hour after hour is unhealthy for your body, your posture, and your eyesight. (Besides which, it can become mind-numbingly boring!)

Figure 1.4   Color Significance Chart

White	Purity, simplicity, cleanliness, sterility, coldness
Gray	Security, reliability, intelligence, dignity, conservativeness, boredom
Red	Excitement, passion, speed, strength, danger, aggression
Yellow	Joy, happiness, optimism, jealousy, deceit
Blue	Trust, confidence, unity, technology, depression
Green	Health, luck, nature, inexperience, misfortune

2

Topic Brainstorming

To determine whether a topic is suitable for you to work with and is potentially profitable, you need to answer the following questions:

- In which topics am I most interested and knowledgeable?
- Does this niche have a large market?
- Does my topic have a future?
- Are there relevant products and services to promote in this niche?
- What competition will I have in this market?
- Does my topic have profit potential?

FOLLOW YOUR PASSION OR CHASE THE MONEY?

Promoting financial services as an affiliate marketer can be hugely lucrative. Merchants pay top-dollar commissions for mortgage, auto, and personal loan application leads.

Example: LowerMyBills.com pays $32 for completed home refinance loan applications and the same for completed inquiries related to home equity loans. In both cases, LowerMyBills.com offers to increase that amount to $40 if an affiliate generates 50 or more "actions" in a particular category.

At the time of publication, E-Loan (eLoan.com) was paying a hefty $150 commission per funded motorcycle loan and $60 to $90 per funded auto purchase loan. Commissions for a qualified mortgage refinance application were between $50 and $75. E-Loan defines a *qualified application* as one with all necessary fields filled in, including a valid name and social security number for a loan product that can be offered by E-Loan or one of its partner lenders.

Talk about easy money! The visitors you refer to E-Loan's site don't have to buy a thing. As long as they can type their correct information into the application form blanks, you should be raking in the big bucks. Goodness knows there's no shortage of demand for credit.

According to Wordtracker's service, more than 500,000 surfers were predicted to search for mortgage-related terms in May 2007, about 500,000 for credit card related terms, while the keyword "loans" topped the charts with well over 1 million searches predicted in the same month. You can find a free trial for Wordtracker's service at http://wordtracker.com. (See Figure 2.1.)

Simply on the basis of commissions paid and market de mand, it might seem that the financial services niche would be a good

Figure 2.1   More Factors to Consider When Choosing a Niche

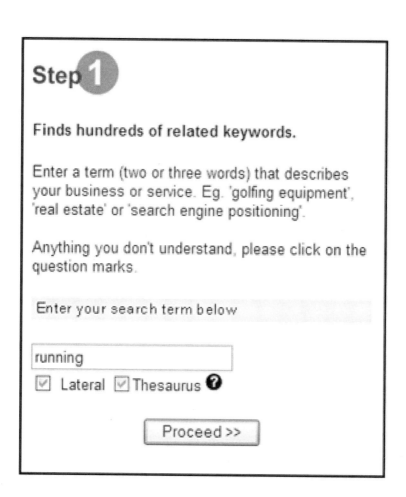

choice for a first affiliate site. However, there are a few more things to consider before you choose to work in such a hot niche. First of all, there are thousands of affiliates already working in the financial services category, making the niche extremely competitive. Second, the cost to advertise and bring traffic to a site in markets with huge demand is very high. At the time of this book's publication, it cost $3.63 to bring just one visitor to your site via Yahoo! Search Marketing's advertising program. Competition and high advertising costs are not the most important considerations, however, because they can be overcome by knowledgeable affiliates.

The most important factor to consider first is your own level of interest and expertise in the topic you choose, because it is very difficult to write about a topic you know nothing about. Affiliates who *chase the money* tend to use the same dry articles and merchant copy that other affiliates have used on their sites. Surfers who see the same information repeated on site after site will not spend much time surveying the site and do not buy recommended products.

It takes time and energy to create a content-rich site that is popular and has credibility with visitors. If you can't fathom writing about debt relief solutions or how to choose a mortgage loan provider in a year from now, you should choose another topic. The main question that needs to be answered is, "Am I really interested in this topic?" In addition, you should be able to answer yes to one or both of the following questions: "Am I knowledgeable about this subject?" and "Am I willing to learn about this topic?"

When you build a site around a topic about which you are knowledgeable or about which you are willing to learn, the result is improved conversion rates—the percentage of visitors who take the desired action—and increased sales. Conversion rates are discussed in more detail in Chapters 7 and 11.

Brainstorm Ideas for Your Topic

Consider the following questions and suggestions to generate a list of possible topics for your site. Make a list of those topics for each question. Then identify the ones in which you are most interested.

- Are you passionate about any subject in particular?
- Do you have expert knowledge in any subject?
- Do you like to read about certain topics more than others?
- Do you have a hobby?
- Are you a collector?
- Are you active in a sport?
- What skills and knowledge have you learned from your jobs, hobbies, and general life experiences?

Do not worry about whether or not there is a market for your topic yet. You will learn how to research demand for your topic later in the book.

In addition to subjects, think about related products that you especially enjoy using and might like to sell online. Name as many subjects as you can think of, but try to come up with a list of 10 to 15 items. Here is a sample subject list:

- Running
- Hiking
- Marathons
- Travel
- Treadmills
- Dogs
- Ceramic dogs

- Animal figurines
- Antique watches

Try to think of specific products that are sold online related to the subjects in your list and jot those down as well. For example, a site about running could sell shoes, treadmills, heart-rate monitors, and clothing for runners. Likewise, in addition to affiliating with Travelocity.com or Expedia.com to earn commissions on travel bookings; a travel site could also offer books, maps, luggage, and electronic translators.

Keep your lists for future reference. After you have built and established your first site, you will return to your lists to get ideas for your second site.

You Don't Have to Be an Expert

Let's assume that you are a keen gardener with a green thumb and discover that "growing indoor plants" is a popular topic online. You know that you have a knack for it, but don't know anything about the technical aspects of indoor gardening.

You believe that there is potential for developing a Web site on indoor gardening—there are the seedlings, plant food, pots, hanging baskets, watering equipment, and plant ornament merchants, just to name a few, you can research as potential affiliate partners. The first steps required in gathering good-quality information for your site content are:

- Buy a book on the subject written by an expert, and read it from cover to cover.
- Visit your local library and grab as many books as you can

on indoor plants, and devour as much relevant information as you can.

- Visit Amazon.com and find at least five books on the subject. Read the comments section and recommendations for more ideas.

- Make a list of the main problems faced by people interested in that topic and the techniques used to solve them.

You should now have all the expertise you need to start writing articles and recommending products to help people solve those problems. Remember, visitors are looking for quality information that will help them find solutions. And you're going to give them that information! You may also discover new ideas related to your topic that you hadn't even thought of.

SUPER AFFILIATE TIP

Do not let the fact that you are not an expert or not passionate about any particular topic dissuade you from becoming an affiliate.

3

Market Research

You may think that tarantulas make the most adorable pets. Before you spend time building an entire site about those cuddly critters, you need to find out whether people share your interest in tarantulas—does a *niche market* really exist?

A *niche* is a group of people who share a common interest. In order for a niche to be worthy of building an affiliate business, it must have significant numbers of people with defined needs and wants that can be met by products or services that those members are willing to purchase.

BROWSERS OR BUYERS—KEYWORDS TELL THE TALE

There are generally three categories of Net surfers looking for information about merchandise, and each type uses different terminology while searching for products online. A word or words that surfers type into the search box at http://Google.com or another search engine is called a *keyword* or *keyword phrase*. For example, a surfer who is looking for a Bose Wave Radio, may type the keyword phrase "Bose Wave Radio" into Google's search box.

You can determine which phase of the buying cycle a surfer is in by understanding the keywords and keyword phrases being used to conduct the search. The first is the *browser* looking for basic information and research. Browsers will use generic keywords like "handbags," "DVDs," "cell phones," "barbecues," and so on. Once they have started to collect information, their search terms will become more specific, as in "designer handbag," "sony dvd," "erickson cell phone," and "char grill barbecue."

By the third stage, you can assume that browsers are primed and ready to buy. They have done their homework, checked out the brands, and have narrowed their search terms down to specific brand names. They will use terms such as "buy Chanel designer handbag," "sony DVP-NS30," "sony ericsson T610," and "char griller smoking pro 580."

This kind of information becomes especially relevant when you are researching primary keyword phrases for specific items that relate to your topic. It will also help you create a logical list of categories and subcategories when you're building your Web site.

USE WORDTRACKER TO RESEARCH DEMAND

Wordtracker is an online keyword generator that builds lists of similar search terms from keywords entered by people who search the Net. Wordtracker also allows affiliates to assess demand for a topic by finding out which keywords surfers search for and how often those keywords are searched. Wordtracker offers a free trial, available at http://Worktracker.com.

To use the service, first build a short list of keywords and keyword phrases that are related to your topic. Your list should include generic terms, product manufacturers, and types of manufacturers. If you are already aware of specific model names or numbers that are popular, include them in your list as well. Let's say that you are an avid runner and that your first choice for a possible affiliate site would be about running. List some of the terms that you, as a runner, would search for if you were doing research online. Your list might look something like this:

Running

Runner

Marathon

Running training

Next list the products that runners might buy, such as:

Running shoes

Heart rate monitors

Training devices

GPS (global positioning systems)

Your manufacturer or company name keyword list may consist of:

Adidas

Asics

Brooks

New Balance

Nike

Saucony

Keyword Research: Generic Terms

To find out how many surfers searched for the keyword "running," go into Wordtracker's interface after signing up for the free trial, and type in the keyword "running." Figure 3.1 shows a partial screen capture of the search results.

As you can see, a number of words related to running were returned by the search, including "marathon," "training," and "running shoes." The benefit of having related keywords show up in the results is that you may get ideas for site topics and subtopics that you may not come up with on your own. This makes Wordtracker an effective brainstorming tool. (Note that the trial version produces only 15 related keywords, whereas the enhanced version would display 285 related terms.

Research Product Types

The eleventh term returned during our search for "running" was the hyperlinked term "running shoes." Clicking on that link produces a list of keywords and keyword phrases on the right side of the interface that includes the term "running shoes" as shown in Figure 3.2.

Brand-Name Research

The list returned for the search on "running shoes," shown in Figure 3.2, is quite informative. It tells us that people are searching for specific brand names such as Nike, Asics, Adidas, and others. Most relevant to our research are the numbers in the column labeled "Predict." This number represents the maximum total predicted traffic for all of the major search engines, pay-per-click search engines, and directories for the current 24-hour period. In this example, the number of predicted searches for the term "Nike running shoes" is 340.

Figure 3.1   Keyword Search Results for "Running"

Step **2**

Click any keyword below
(to search our database of metacrawler queries.
Results will appear in the right window)

Related keywords for running

Why do I need related keywords? Click here

1.   running

2.   training

3.   run

4.   runner

5.   marathon

6.   runners

7.   fitness

8.   jogging

9.   race

10.   calendar

11.   running shoes

12.   program

13.   exercise

14.   jog

15.   joggers

The enhanced version would display 285 keywords here.

(If the above keywords are irrelevant, please use the back button
in your browser and try a different keyword)

Figure 3.2   Keyword Search Results for "Running Shoes"

Click on keywords below
to add to basket

Searching...100 row(s) returned

Taken from all Dogpile & Metacrawler queries over the last 90 days.

Your trial results have been filtered to remove adult words.

Click here to add all keywords to your basket			
Keyword (?)	Count (?)	Predict (?)	Dig (?)
running shoes	894	1577	✎
nike running shoes	193	340	✎
brooks running shoes	136	240	✎
new balance running shoes	124	219	✎
asics running shoes	106	187	✎
adidas running shoes	75	132	✎
best running shoes	67	118	✎
discount running shoes	67	118	✎
trail running shoes	61	108	✎
saucony running shoes	44	78	✎
puma running shoes	41	72	✎
track running shoes	33	58	✎
mizuno running shoes	31	55	✎
discount new balance running shoes	25	44	✎
vintage puma running shoes	22	39	✎

The other 85 keywords are available
in the enhanced version!

The results should give you some idea of where to concentrate your product promotional efforts. For example, you would dig a little deeper and search for each individual brand name using the Wordtracker. A search for "Nike" yielded the results shown in Figure 3.3.

At this point, keep searching for Nike products to see whether any particular model of Nike is more sought after than others. During the search for the keyword "Nike," the term "nike air shox" was returned in the fifth spot with 1734 searches predicted for the day. A search for "Nike Shox" yielded the results shown in Figure 3.4.

According to the number of searches shown in Figure 3.4, it appears that the Nike Shox Turbo is the most popular Nike Shox shoe, followed by Shox R4 and TL models. Each of these terms should be added to your keyword list as you continue to research your topic.

Unfortunately, there is no definitive answer as to how many searches makes a topic worthwhile to pursue as an affiliate marketing business. Some webmasters prefer to work only in very large markets that receive at least 500,000 searches per month on a very generic term.

Example: The keyword "Dating" was predicted to receive 8610 searches on May 23, 2007 according to the keyword selector tool. If you add the 9362 searches for "singles" that were predicted for the same day, you now have over 557,000 searches predicted for terms related to dating. That indicates a huge market.

Huge markets are however very competitive and expensive to advertise in. Therefore, some webmasters prefer to find a smaller niche in which advertising costs may be lower and the subsequent return on their advertising investment is higher. That said, most super affiliates are willing to invest their efforts in any topic that returns about 100,000 searches in any given month for a generic term related to the subject.

Figure 3.3   Keyword Search Results for "Nike"

Click here to add **all** keywords to your basket			
Keyword (?)	**Count** (?)	**Predict** (?)	**Dig** (?)
nike	5904	10413	✎
nike shoes	1649	2908	✎
nike basketball camps	1182	2085	✎
nike logo	994	1753	✎
nike shox	983	1734	✎
nike dunks	578	1019	✎
nike air force 1	489	862	✎
nikes	435	767	✎
nike golf	407	718	✎
nike swoosh	290	511	✎
nike air force ones	283	499	✎
nike basketball	243	429	✎
nike air force one	238	420	✎
nike soccer balls	225	397	✎

Figure 3.4   Keyword Search Results for "Nike Shox"

Click here to add **all** keywords to your basket			
Keyword (?)	**Count** (?)	**Predict** (?)	**Dig** (?)
nike shox	983	1734	✎
nike shox turbo	77	136	✎
nike shox r4	53	93	✎
nike shox tl	39	69	✎
nike shox respond	38	67	✎
nike shox cl	35	62	✎
nike shox navina	34	60	✎
womens nike shox	34	60	✎
nike shox junga	33	58	✎
nike shox turbo oz	33	58	✎
nike shox disobey	32	56	✎
nike shox nz	31	55	✎
nike shox shoes	30	53	✎

In searching for only four keywords—running, running shoes, Nike, and Nike Shox—we saw that in just one month, 19,394 searches were predicted for those terms in one day, or approximately 600,000 searches for the month.

There are many more search engines, including Google.com, people use to search for information online. Therefore, the numbers of people interested in the topic of running and who are doing related research online is substantial.

YOUR KEYWORD LIST: THE BIGGER THE BETTER

As you research your topic, keep building a list of keywords that are relevant to your topic. Your keyword list will eventually be used to create focused content and drive traffic to your site using pay-per-click search engine advertising. Building a list of keywords that includes the number of searches for each keyword and phrase will make it easy for you to know on which categories and products you should concentrate your efforts. Your goal is to create a huge keyword list that includes your topic's categories and subcategories as well as brand, product names, and model numbers, if applicable.

Try to think like your potential customers and search for keywords that they might use. If you were doing research for a niche site about running, search for terms such as "runner" and "run" in addition to the term "running." Use misspellings, contractions, and any other forms of the words you can think of to build out your list. Terms that are returned by your search such as "running shoes," "pedometer," "10K," and others will give you ideas to broaden the scope of your site and the products you choose to sell.

Figure 3.5 contains a sample keyword list for a site about running. The list was built using the related keyword search through Wordtracker.com.

Figure 3.5 Sample Keyword List for Running Site

10K	races
10k run	racing
5K	REFLECTIVE CLOTHING
5k race	run
5k run	runner
800 meters	runners
ADIDAS RUNNING SHOES	running
AIF	running a marathon
Arkansas running clubs	RUNNING ACCESSORIES
ASICS RUNNING SHOES	running advice
athletics	RUNNING APPAREL
BABY JOGGERS	running apparel
Bass	RUNNING CLOTHES
beginners running	running clothing
BROOKS RUNNING SHOES	running club
brooks running shoes	running clubs
brooks running socks	running events
CD	running exercise
cross country	running fitness
CROSS COUNTRY SHOES	RUNNING JACKET
discount running shoes	RUNNING PANTS
etonic running shoes	RUNNING RACES
event calendar	running shoes
exercise	RUNNING SHORTS

(continued)

Figure 3.5 (continued)

field	RUNNING SOCKS
fitness	RUNNING STORES
GAIT ANALYSIS	running technique
HEART RATE MONITORS	SALOMON TRAIL SHOES
HYDRATION SYSTEMS	SAUCONY RUNNING SHOES
London marathon	SUN GLASSES
marathon	track
MIZUNO RUNNING SHOES	TRACK SHOES
NATHAN REFLECTIVE GEAR	TRACK SPIKES
NEW BALANCE RUNNING SHOES	TRAIL SHOES
NIKE RUNNING SHOES	training
PEDOMETERS	Video
POLAR HEART RATE MONITORS	VIDEO GAIT ANALYSIS
race	workouts
race calendar	

As you "drill down" through individual terms that are relevant to your proposed topic, your list will continue to grow in size and scope.

DOES MY TOPIC HAVE A FUTURE?

You do not want to find out that interest in the product or service you are trying to sell is decreasing after you have built your site. To evaluate and stay current on trends in the market, read the newspaper and relevant magazines and do online research. Good sources of information about online spending are comScore Networks (comscore.com) and the Online Publishers Association (OPA) (online-publishers.org).

According to an August 2, 2006, comScore Networks press release, several retail categories achieved significant growth during the first half of 2006 compared to the previous year. Office supplies, which saw online spending rise by 54 percent, were reported as the top-gaining retail category. Computer software grew by 39 percent, sports and fitness was up by 38 percent, home and garden rose by 36 percent, and toys and hobbies increased by 33 by percent. If the topic you have chosen for your site involves selling office supplies or computer software; or is in the sports and fitness, home and garden, or toys and hobbies categories, you might be jumping for joy right now. If your topic is not one of those listed, do not give up hope. There are a number of market and trend information sources online. Here are just a few:

- *comScore Media* (http://www.comscore.com) claims to have 'the largest consumer measurement system of its kind to deliver insight and expertise in the following industries: automotive, travel, pharmaceutical, retail, financial services, telecommunications, media, entertainment, and consumer packaged goods.

- *Forrester Research* (http://www.forrester.com) surveys 250,000 consumers every year in 15 countries to uncover purchasing and spending habits, technology adoption trends, customer demand, and buyer attitudes. Guest registration gives access to free research.

- *Jupiter Research* (http://www.jupiterresearch.com) provides unbiased research, analysis, and advice, backed by proprietary data, to help companies profit from the impact of the Internet and emerging consumer technologies on their business. You may register as a guest for access to sample research and special features like personalized e-mail alerts and a personal research library.

- *Online Publishers Association* (http://www.online-publishers. org) is a not-for-profit industry trade organization that produces research concerning online advertising and media consumption with the goal of advancing the online publishing industry.

- *ClickZ Network* (http://www.clickz.com) supplies news, information, commentary, advice, opinion, research, and reference related to interactive marketing. You will find in-depth profiles, interviews, case studies, and features on cutting-edge products, companies, and trends.

- *PRWeb.com* (http://prweb.com) is one of the largest online press release newswires. Users may search news by category, country, metropolitan statistical area (MSA), day, or trackbacks. (A *trackback* is a mechanism for communication between Web blogs, or blogs. You may search prweb.com by trackbacks to see which press releases have most recently been commented upon throughout the blogsphere, or to find out which press release has received the most comments.)

- *eBay Marketplace Research* (http://pages.ebay.com/market place_research) was introduced in late 2005 to help buyers and sellers track transaction trends on eBay. The service provides average item prices, shows top keyword searches by category or related keywords, creates charts illustrating transaction trends, and delivers data on completed sales over the past 90 days. Marketplace Research is subscription-based and comes in three tiers, starting at $2.99 for two days of access.

In addition, both Google.com and Yahoo! News offer free news alerts. By providing relevant keywords or key phrases, Google and Yahoo! News will download all the news stories on your topic of interest direct to your e-mail account daily.

SUPER AFFILIATE TIP

Do your homework and evaluate trends in your potential market before you choose your final niche topic. Research demand through Yahoo! Search Marketing and Wordtracker, and find out what is hot according to PRWeb, Google News, eBay, and research companies such as comScore and Jupiter Networks. As the old saying goes, "Success is 90 percent planning and 10 percent execution."

4

Find and Choose Products
to Promote

Now that you have found a niche with sufficient demand, you will want to confirm that merchants offer products within that niche and that they have affiliate programs for you to join. Affiliate programs can be found listed through affiliate networks, independent merchant sites, and affiliate program directories.

AFFILIATE NETWORKS

As online advertising gets more competitive, complicated, and expensive, Web merchants increasingly promote their products through affiliate networks.

Affiliate networks act as third-party bona fide brokers and function as intermediaries between merchants and affiliates. Merchants use affiliate networks to list their products and the details of their affiliate programs, and affiliates can apply to those merchants they are interested in and for whose programs they qualify.

Figure 4.1 lists major product categories and subcategories within the Commission Junction (CJ.com) network. It gives you an idea of some of the affiliate products you can sell via this network.

Joining an affiliate network places thousands of eager affiliates right on the doorstep of merchants. The marketing value and simplicity to a company of having another company administer its affiliate program is worth the (sometimes) hefty fees charged by the networks.

Joining an affiliate network is free for affiliates, and the process of finding and selecting programs is simplified through categorical search facilities. Because merchants pay top dollar for a good network's management services, affiliate networks in general tend to offer higher-quality programs. Being able to access your statistics in a centralized interface is another big benefit of joining a network. It is a win-win situation for merchants and affiliates.

Each affiliate network is set up and operates differently. Networks generally handle sales tracking statistics and provision of marketing tools. Most networks consolidate affiliates' earnings into a single monthly paycheck. To join most networks, you enter all your contact and payment details (name, address, phone number, etc.) just once. After your application is accepted, you can apply to each merchant's program separately. In some instances, approval is immediate, and in others you may have to wait a day (or seven) for the merchant to get back to you.

Marketing material for each merchant is readily available, and your affiliate linking codes can usually be created with a single mouse click. You simply cut and paste the code into your Web site pages. Banners are usually hosted on the network's servers, saving

Figure 4.1   Commission Junction Product and Service Categories

Category	Products
Auto	Accessories, Cars, Rentals
Business and Career	B-To-B (Business-to-Business, Employment, Real Estate)
Clothing and Accessories	Accessories, Children, Jewelry, Men, Women
Computer and Electronics	Consumer, Hardware, Software
Department Store	Clothing, Gifts, Home, Jewelry
Entertainment	Books/Magazines, Music, Videos
Family	Baby, Education, Entertainment, Pets
Financial Services	Banking/Trading, Credit Cards, Loans
Food and Drink	Candy, Cigars, Gourmet, Wine
Games and Toys	Children, Educational, Electronic
Gift and Flowers	Flowers, Gifts, Greeting Cards
Health and Beauty	Bath/Body, Cosmetics, Medical Supplies and Services, Prescriptions, Vitamins
Hobbies and Collectibles	Art, Auctions, Collectibles
Home and Living	Bed/Bath, Garden, Improvement, Kitchen
Internet and Online	Development, Hosting, Online Dating, Programs, Services
Mature/Adult	Apparel, Books, Entertainment

(Continued)

Figure 4.1 (Continued)

Category	Products
Office	Equipment, Home Office, Supplies
Sports and Fitness	Clothing, Collectibles, Equipment
Telecommunications	Equipment, Long Distance, Wireless
Travel	Airline, Car, Hotel, Vacations

you money when you exceed the amount of bandwidth allowed by your Internet hosting account. Bandwith is the amount of data that is transferred within a given period of time.

A few major affiliate networks are:

- *Commission Junction* (CJ.com) *Linkshare.com* and *Performics.com* are the major affiliate networks.
- *ShareaSale.com* is a smaller, but very popular network with affiliates.
- *Clickbank.com* specializes in digital products and has a built-in affiliate network.

(See Appendixes A and B for more detailed information about the affiliate networks named above and a list of 38 additional networks.)

SEARCH GOOGLE FOR INDEPENDENT MERCHANTS

If you have not been able to find a merchant with an affiliate program that sells the type products you want to promote, here is a search technique that will help you locate exactly what you are looking for.

For example, if you wanted to sell Barbie dolls and Barbie accessories, you would visit Google and type "+Barbie +doll +affiliate" into the search box. Do not include the quotes, but do include the plus signs. The plus signs ensure that each word entered appears on the pages returned in the search results. However, the pages returned are not guaranteed to have a Barbie doll accessories affiliate program. Some of the sites may be affiliates themselves, but looking around their site should give you clues as to the identity of the merchant. Other sites that are returned by your search will in fact be merchant sites.

While reviewing individual sites and pages, look for links on the site that say, "webmasters," "make money," "affiliate (or associate) program," "partners," "earn $," and other phrases that indicate that the company has an affiliate program.

AFFILIATE PROGRAM DIRECTORIES

Affiliate program directories are Web sites that contain lists of links to affiliate programs that have been compiled and organized by various webmasters. Affiliate program directories can be used to find merchants that have stand-alone or "in-house" programs that are not associated with the big affiliate networks.

Programs are typically categorized by product type (e.g., educational, business, etc.) and include brief summaries of each program with sufficient information to allow affiliates to choose which programs they would like to join. Some also provide program ratings supplied by program users.

When you are searching through the directories, you will discover that many of the merchants listed are also affiliated with networks like Commission Junction and Performics. Therefore, research the networks first because in all likelihood you will be redirected back to them anyway to sign up for many of the programs.

Although there are hundreds of affiliate program directories, listed below are two of the most popular, as well as a site that offers a list of directories.

- *AssociatePrograms.com.* With over 9,000 program listings, AssociatePrograms.com offers the most comprehensive list of affiliate programs anywhere on the Net. The site is easy to use, and listings appear alphabetically in the search results, making it easy to locate programs again later. Listings include commission structure information and brief product descriptions. If you have firsthand experience with any of the programs listed, you are invited to share your two cents' worth and rate the program.

- *Refer-it.com.* This is a division of Internet.com and has listings that are more detailed than those at AssociatePrograms. com and includes the launch date and number of affiliates.

- *PartnerIndustry.com* (http://www.partnerindustry.com/ adirectories.htm). Offers a list of directories.

Join Commission Junction

To find out which merchants offer products through Commission Junction, you must join its network at CJ.com. A screen capture of the homepage is shown in Figure 4.2.

Once you are on the homepage, place your cursor over the word "Publishers," and then click on "Application" which will take you to the application form page shown in Figure 4.3.

Figure 4.2 Commission Junction Homepage

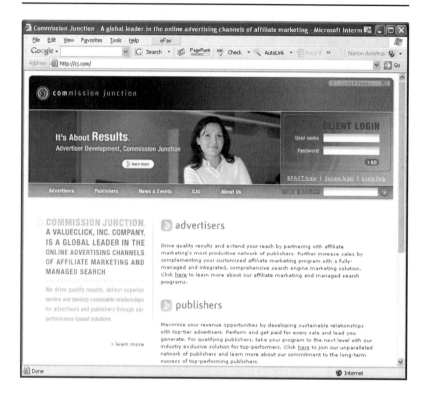

During the sign-up process, you will be asked to provide your Web site or newsletter name, URL, and a description of your site or newsletter contents. Simply put in a newsletter name and a brief description for now. You will be able to change and add sites to your profile later.

Once you have established an account, click on "Get Links" from the homepage. Figure 4.4 shows you how the interface will appear on your screen.

Figure 4.3   Commission Junction Application

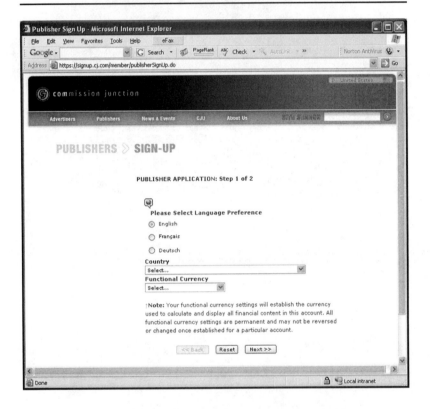

You can search by category, or type a product or company name into the search box to find products. When you click on "sports" within the category list, all the merchants with sporting goods are displayed on the screen, as shown in a partial screen capture in Figure 4.5.

Check out each of the merchant offers in your category, and see how the commission rates compare to one another.

Figure 4.4 Commission Junction "Get Links" Interface

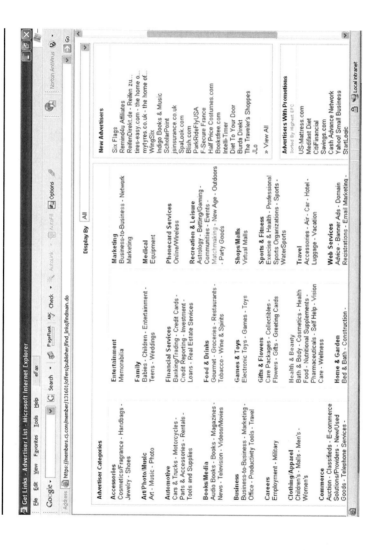

Figure 4.5 Commission Junction Category Search Results for "Sports"

Get Links - Advertiser List - Microsoft Internet Explorer

File Edit View Favorites Tools Help   eFax

Google ▼ | Search ▼ | PageRank | Check ▼ | AutoLink | AutoFill | Options | Norton AntiVirus

Address https://members.cj.com/member/131601/publisher/offers/search/getlinks.do?findItem=advertiser&default=no&displayby=&categoryId=372 Go

Advertiser Search Results

Results 1 - 25 of 64   «Previous 1 | 2 | 3 Next»

Apply to Program   Select All

Advertiser	3 Month EPC (USD)	7 Day EPC (USD)	Network Earnings	Sale	Lead	Click	Status	Category
SmoothFitness.com » View Links » View Products	$108.83	$127.08		Sale: 8.00% USD			Active	Exercise & Health
Dinn Bros. Trophies » View Links » View Products	$59.94	$31.47		Sale: 6.00% USD Performance Incentive			No Relationship	Sports
Overtons.com » View Links	$50.06	$32.10		Sale: 4.00% USD			No Relationship	WaterSports
Baseball Express » View Links	$49.59	$44.92		Sale: 8.00% USD			No Relationship	Sports
Denise Austin Fit Forever » View Links	$42.61	$40.71		Sale: $30.00 USD Performance Incentive			No Relationship	Exercise & Health
REI » View Links » View Products	$41.96	$35.94		Sale: 5.00% USD			No Relationship	Outdoors
Hockey Giant » View Links	$40.11	$28.99		Sale: 7.00% USD			No Relationship	Sports
StubHub.com » View Links » View Products	$38.82	$75.79		Sale: 8.00% USD			Active	Entertainment
Zappos.com » View Links » View	$37.43	$60.72		Sale: 15.00% USD Performance Incentive			Active	Shoes

Done   Local intranet

In Figure 4.6 individual products are shown for a search for "running." Note that the product image, name, relevant catalog, price, and company selling the product are listed in each row.

Do not break out the calculator yet. We are still in the research phase and will return to the subject of joining affiliate programs later.

DO YOU REALLY WANT TO PROMOTE THAT PRODUCT?

Promoting quality products offered by reputable merchants is crucial to the success of your affiliate business. However, product quality and merchant reputation should not be your only concerns when it comes to choosing products for your site. We have all seen sites that display ads for products that are not relevant to a site's content. For example, ads for contact lens cleaner on a site about kids' room decor look out of place and are a distraction to visitors. If you really must sell contact lens cleaner, consider starting a site about vision care instead.

Having firsthand knowledge about the products you promote gives you an edge over other affiliates selling the same product. You build credibility and trust with your customers when you can talk about products from experience. Although the price of costly items may prohibit actual purchases, you can often still try the product out at a store. For example, if you sell treadmills, visit a local fitness equipment store and try out the various models. Make note of your experience and report what you experienced.

For less expensive products, you may be able to purchase an item through your own affiliate link. If the commission rate on that item was 50 percent, you would then need to make only one more sale to get your money back and start making a profit. As an affiliate, you do not want to get e-mail from your merchant's customers

Figure 4.6 Commission Junction Product Search Results for "Running"

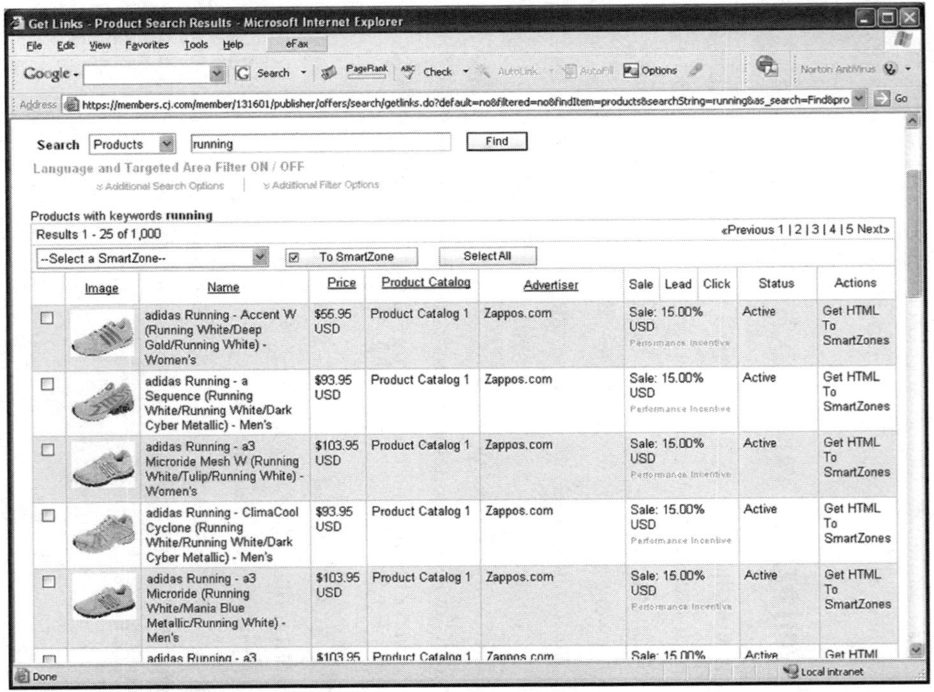

because the company is not responding to its customer service enquiries. So if you buy a product from a company you are unfamiliar with, check out its customer service. Make sure that its response is both quick and effective. Most merchants promise a response within 24 to 48 hours of receiving an inquiry; however, many reply more quickly. Let your visitors know if the customer service provided by a particular merchant is exemplary.

Online Shoppers Are Price Sensitive

Compare prices on the same or similar products at a number of different online stores. You should try to offer your customers goods at the lowest prices through programs that offer the best commission rates. Although finding this situation requires extra research, the effort will be well worth the reward.

Is the company's site attractive and functional? Would you buy from a site that looked unprofessional, had broken links, or was a hassle to navigate? Do not send your visitors to tacky sites. Your reputation is at stake.

SUPER AFFILIATE TIP

Look for products and services to promote at affiliate networks, directories, and merchants' in-house programs. However, resist the temptation to sign up for programs until your Web site is in place because merchants are generally unwilling to accept applications from webmasters with incomplete sites.

5

Research the Competition

Now that you know that there is sufficient demand for your chosen topic and that merchants have relevant products available through affiliate programs, it is time to research the competition.

REVIEW NATURAL, OR ORGANIC, SEARCH ENGINE RESULTS

We begin by reviewing the organic, or natural, search results. To continue with our "running" theme, we type the word "running" into the search box at Google, and the results appear as shown in the screen capture in Figure 5.1. Organic results are those outlined.

As you can see from the screen capture, nearly 1.5 billion results were returned for the word "running." When you see large numbers like that returned, you might conclude that there is no point in building a site about running because it will never be able to compete with

Figure 5.1   Google Search Results for "Running"

such a vast number of sites. Do not be intimidated by large numbers of natural search engine results, however. Although the number of natural listings is generally a good indicator of interest in a subject, the number of results returned for a particular keyword or keyword phrase is largely a very poor indicator of actual competition for a number of reasons.

Organic results on generic terms may not be relevant. "Running" is a very generic word. Some, if not most, of the pages that contain the term "running" may in fact be about other topics. Examples include references to the movie *Running Scared* or sites that sell "running boards" for trucks. Indeed, a search for "Running Scared" at Google returned over 4 million pages containing that particular phrase, and "running boards" returned nearly 2 million results. If you were to review a number of terms that are popularly used with the word "running," you would find that the number of e-commerce sites related to running as a sport is nothing to be worried about.

Organic search engine results are unstable and change often. Google is constantly tweaking its algorithms, which determines which sites qualify to rank near the top of its natural search listings.

Sites that are ranked first today may suddenly be shown in the 50th spot or disappear from the listings altogether tomorrow. Organic results may not offer the most recent information.

It appears that Google gives precedence to sites and pages in which a particular topic appeared first and will rank those sites higher. However, as you research a topic, you will often discover that the information on that site or those pages has become out of date or, on occasion, the pages have been removed from the site, and you will receive a "404–page not found" error. Those pages surely do not qualify as competition!

People will not work all that hard to obtain information on the Internet. Would you search through page after page until you had seen 1.5 billion results for the word "running"? Most surfers visit only those sites that are listed on the first or second page of Google returns. That tendency essentially makes the other 1,4999,999,980 sites irrelevant.

The best use of organic results is to see how others in the industry promote their products and to get some idea of how you can to do it better.

Research the Paid or Sponsored Listings

To find out which sites qualify as competition, you need to evaluate those sites that pay to advertise. More specifically, research who uses pay-per-click (PPC) advertising to promote their sites. Pay-per-click advertising is a type of search marketing in which advertisers bid for placement in the search results and pay each and every time their ad is clicked. Yahoo! Search Marketing and Google Adwords are two examples of many companies that offer pay-per-click search engine advertising.

You can review the average cost-per-click and search volume for ads appearing for your keywords using the Google Adwords Keyword Tool at https://adwords.google.com/select/KeywordTool.

To see the estimated ad position and estimates of how much advertisers are bidding on the keyword "running," enter the term into the box, select "Cost and Ad Position Estimates" from the drop-down and enter the maximum CPC (cost-per-click) you would be willing to bid on your keywords. (See Figure 5.2.) Hint: Place a high value in the maximum CPC to see more returns.

Figure 5.3 shows which advertisers are bidding on the term "running" as well as the amount of their maximum bid for that keyword. The maximum bid is located at the bottom of each listing. Notice that each ad consists of an ad title, ad description, site URL and, last, the advertiser's max bid.

As you can see in Figure 5.3, the estimated cost-per-click to achieve an estimated ad position between first and third place on Google Adwords for the term "running shoe" is $1.64. The plural form is estimated to cost $2.01.

Figure 5.2   Google Adwords Keyword Tool

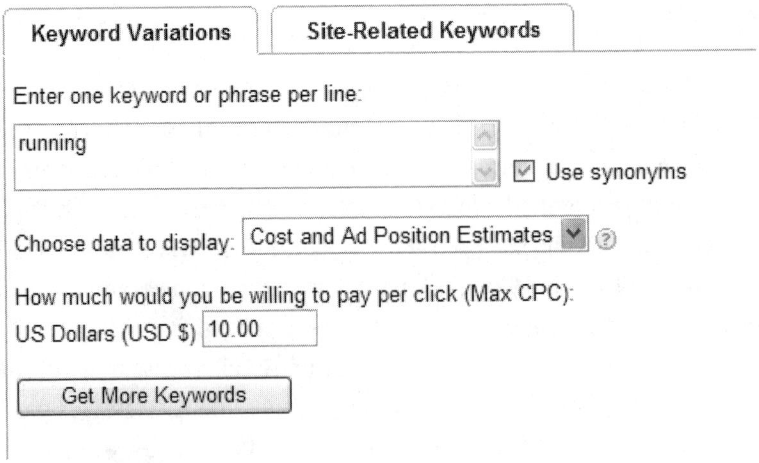

Figure 5.3   Google Adwords Keyword Tool Results for "Running"

Keywords	Estimated Avg. CPC	Estimated Ad Position	Match Type: ⑦ Broad ▾
running shoe	$1.64	1 - 3	Add »
running shoes	$2.01	1 - 3	Add »
marathon running	$0.98	1 - 3	Add »
running training	$1.33	1 - 3	Add »
running gear	$2.03	1 - 3	Add »
running shorts	$1.71	1 - 3	Add »
trail running	$1.70	1 - 3	Add »
running clothes	$1.89	1 - 3	Add »
running store	$1.32	1 - 3	Add »
running	$1.34	1 - 3	Add »
brooks running	$2.10	1 - 3	Add »
running 5k	$0.75	1 - 3	Add »
adidas running	$1.35	1 - 3	Add »
running clothing	$2.30	1 - 3	Add »
running fitness	$1.46	1 - 3	Add »
running apparel	$2.18	1 - 3	Add »
running jogging	$1.05	1 - 3	Add »
women's running	$1.81	1 - 3	Add »
running times	$0.57	1 - 3	Add »
running marathons	$0.67	1 - 3	Add »

We can easily count the number of advertisers (36) bidding on the keyword term "running" by going to Overture.com, entering the term, and then counting the number of sponsored listings as shown circled in Figure 5.4.

Figure 5.4 Yahoo! Search Marketing Total Number of Advertisers

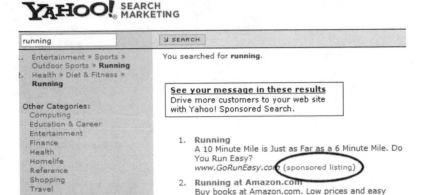

Now let's take a look at webmasters who are advertising on Google. Google's sponsored listings are located at the top of the search results page, while Google Adwords are on the right side of each results page, as shown in Figure 5.5.

You can get a good idea of how many advertisers are bidding on individual keywords and keyword phrases through Google Adwords by clicking on "More Sponsored Links" at the bottom of the Adwords column. Eight advertisers' listings are listed on the first page of results, and ten are listed per page on all subsequent results pages.

Example: You searched for "running shoes" at Google, and then clicked on the more sponsored links and saw that there were two full pages of advertisers and that the third page, yup! had only four

Figure 5.5   Google Sponsored Links

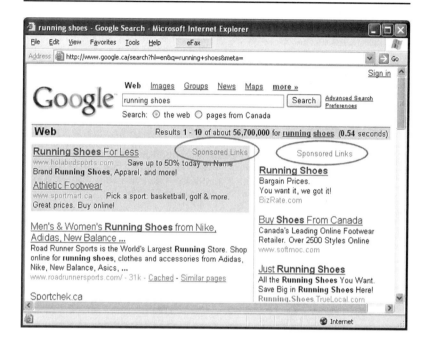

listings. That would mean there were a total of 32 advertisers bidding on the term "running shoes."

Do Affiliates Compete in This Niche?

What you really want to know is whether affiliates are using pay-per-click advertising to promote their sites. If they are paying for advertising, it is a relatively safe bet that their sites are generating a profit and that therefore the subject you have chosen is a potentially profitable niche. To find affiliate advertisers, add the words "guide," "review," or "comparison" to your search term. For example, Figure 5.6 shows

Figure 5.6   Results for "Running Shoes Comparison" Search

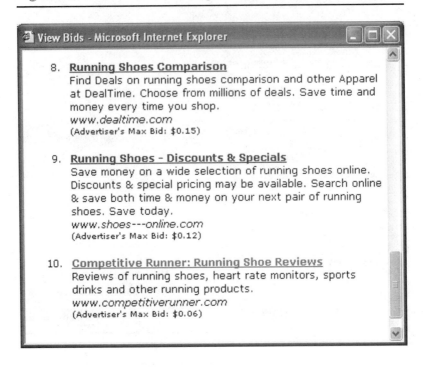

results for a search for "running shoes comparison" at Yahoo! Search Marketing, or Overture.com.

The search returned 30 sponsored listings. The majority of advertisers were the big shopping comparison sites such as Shopzilla.com, Nextag.com, Bizrate.com, and Dealtime.com. Although these sites earn revenue through their affiliations with online merchants, most also have their own affiliate programs.

These large comparison sites are sometimes referred to as first-tier affiliates, because they have a direct relationship with the merchant. If you join a first-tier affiliate's affiliate program, in essence you become a second-tier affiliate. In Chapter 9, "Choose and Join Affiliate Programs," the advantages and disadvantages of joining such programs are discussed.

Big players like the huge comparison sites have ample advertising budgets. What you are looking for are mom-and-pop types of affiliate operations that operate directly with merchants and are advertising their sites in the pay-per-click search engines.

In some cases you will find a smaller affiliate whose only income from the site is earned through Google Adsense, rather than from affiliate programs. Google Adsenser's are easy to spot because their sites typically show Google Adwords prominently on every page of their sites, such as the example shown in Figure 5.7.

Figure 5.7 Google Adsense Affiliate

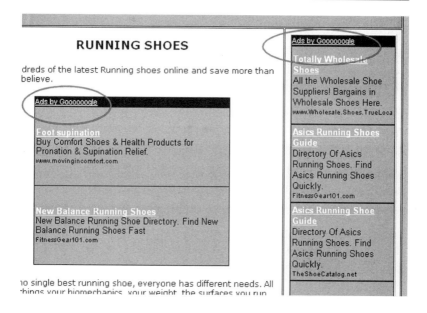

Figure 5.8   CompetitiveRunner.com

11. **Running Shoes Review**
    Find and Compare prices on running shoes review at Smarter.com.
    www.*smarter.com* (sponsored listing)

12. **The Men's Guide to Shoes**
    Where To Shop & 8 Shoe Terms You Should Know. Read "The Guide" Now.
    www.*esquire.com* (sponsored listing)

13. **Competitive Runner: Running Shoe Reviews**
    Resource for competitive runners. Find reviews of running shoes, heart rate monitors,
    sports drinks and other running products.
    www.*competitiverunner.com* (sponsored listing)

14. **Running Shoe Review**
    That should be the mantra for every person who works in a running shoe store. ... The
    following running shoe review ranks the top five shoes costing $100 or less. ...
    www.*healthandfitnessmag.com* (additional listing)

Sites made for Adsense have very few affiliate links that go directly to a merchant's product pages, so we would continue our search for affiliates that promote merchants' products. (Earning through Google Adsense is discussed in a later chapter.)

The listing in the thirteenth spot went to CompetitiveRunner. com, shown in Figure 5.8. The paid link from Yahoo! Search Marketing went directly to a page that had a comparison chart for a number of different shoes for road running.

"Shop" links from the comparison review page at Competitive Runner.com direct visitors to RoadRunnerSports.com. RoadRunner Sports.com is a merchant with an affiliate program through the Performics.com affiliate network. An affiliate site like Compet itiveRunner.com is exactly the type of site to look for when you are researching a potential niche.

Do not stop looking after you have found one affiliate site using pay-per-click advertising in your niche. Find more affiliate sites by taking your primary keywords and adding words such as:

Articles

Buying guide

Comparison

Directories

Guide

Resources

Review

Tips

Tricks

Example: You can search Google.com for "running shoe review," "runner's resources," and "running shoe guide" to find affiliate sites advertising in your proposed niche.

Is the Competition Relevant?

As you research your proposed topic, a variety of sites will show up in the results, including competing affiliates, merchant sites, and sites that are irrelevant to your subject. The primary objective in reviewing these sites is to find merchants with great products and affiliate programs, as well as good ideas for your site.

It is also good to find affiliates who bid high for certain keyword phrases, yet whose sites are somehow lacking. For example, you may discover an affiliate who pays to display its listing in the second spot on the results page for the term "cell phone reviews." When you visit the site, you might see that all it displays "above the fold" are Google Adsense listings, which typically earn only pennies per click. "Above the fold" refers to that portion of the Web site that is visible without scrolling down the page.

Instead of earning pennies per click, a smarter affiliate would offer well-written product endorsements for phone sales and plans merchants. For example, LetsTalk.com pays $45 per phone sale and offers to increase commissions by 40 percent when sales equal or exceed 30 units in any given month.

You will find yourself both surprised and delighted to discover that sites paying the most to advertise are often poorly designed or do not offer a wide range of products relevant to the keywords they are advertising. In those cases, if you build a well-designed Web site that gives the surfers exactly what they want, your site should be successful, even if you do not list it in a top spot on the pay-per-click search engines.

Do not overlook this step in your affiliate business-building process. You will be surprised at how much you will learn by researching the competition. In many cases, you will be pleasantly surprised to see how little competition there is and how much room the market holds—just for you.

CHOOSE YOUR NICHE

Now that you have researched one or more topics in which you are particularly interested, it is time to choose a topic and start working on your Web site. Do not wait to find the "perfect topic." It does not exist. There will always be some little problem or weakness with whatever niche you choose. Choose the best among those you researched, or continue researching until you find the one that suits you best.

SUPER AFFILIATE TIP

As you gain experience, your site will grow and evolve over time into something much larger and better than you ever hoped or expected. Be patient and give yourself time.

6

Plan Your Site

New webmasters seem to think that building a portal site or "super mall" that sells every type of product under the sun will save them the work of having to build multiple sites and that it is the fastest way to online riches. Unfortunately, e-commerce and affiliate marketing do not work that way.

KEEP IT SUPER SIMPLE

If you search for ways to earn money online, you would probably visit Google.com and type in phrases such as "make money," "make money online," and "work at home." The sites returned would likely be specific to the phrase that you searched. That is the benefit of using search engines like Google and pay-per-click search engines like Yahoo! Search Marketing. The results returned are highly relevant to your search, which saves you time, effort, and frustration. Customers are no different in their desire to find specific, highly relevant information on the Web. They too want to save their time and effort and get highly relevant results when they are surfing the Web. That means building theme sites, or sites that are focused on a single topic.

SUPER AFFILIATE TIP

Customer satisfaction must be the first goal of any business—including your affiliate marketing business.

Focus on your customers first and foremost, and the few extra dollars you spend to build individual theme sites will be more than offset when happy customers support your sites with their dollars.

The opposite of the mall approach is to build multiple sites, all around the same theme or topic. This approach is also a waste of time, effort, and money. Building three different sites that promote the same products does not make sense because the sites are competing with one another. Furthermore, if you use Google Adwords and Yahoo! Search Marketing to advertise your sites, you may use a keyword or keyword phrase only once per account.

If you have 10 sites about digital camcorders, how would you decide which site to send surfers who typed in the keyword phrase "digital camcorder"? Building multiple sites around the same theme works only when you make a clear distinction between the products offered. For example, you may have three domains offering three different categories of online dating services. They could be categorized as mild, medium, and hot; in other words, nonadult, mixed, and adult. With distinctive sites, it is easier to know to which site to send the surfer who wants to see "adult dating sites" as opposed to "pen pals."

AFFILIATE SITE MODELS

There are as many different ways to build an affiliate Web site as there are affiliates. Some sites consist of only one page, while others have tens of thousands of pages. The most commonly used affiliate site models include:

- Content/product review sites
- Comparison sites
- Coupon, discount, price drop, and deal-of-day sites
- Hybrid sites

Content/Product Review Sites

The emphasis in content/product review sites is on giving visitors plenty of free information about a particular topic and then gently leading them to reviews of relevant products that solve specific problems. Continuing with our "running" theme, more mature runners and those in intensive training may wonder whether they should be using a heart rate monitor.

Your webmaster could answer that question in an article titled "Runners: Should You Use a Heart Rate Monitor?" or "The Case for and against Heart Rate Monitors." At the end of the article, the webmaster would include a related information section that leads to product reviews

Figure 6.1   Related Information

For more information about heart rate monitors, please visit "Heart Rate Monitors Reviewed" in the Gadgets section of our site. See individual heart rate monitors from Polar, Reebok, Timex®, and other suppliers compared side by side.

---

of selected heart rate monitors. Figure 6.1 provides an example of how to introduce a product relevant to the topic of an article.

"Heart Rate Monitors Reviewed" mentioned in Figure 6.1 will link to a page named "heart-rate-monitors-reviewed.html." On that page, the webmaster could include a subcategory list of heart rate monitor manufacturers that he or she has reviewed. Alternatively, if only a few different products have been reviewed, links may go directly to product review pages. Each link to a product page might also include a short description of the product. The product list may be ordered either alphabetically or by rank, if a rating system has been developed.

Figure 6.2 is an abbreviated example of a product subcategory page. Note that the header and navigation elements have been eliminated from this example.

Each underlined phrase such as "Timex Heart Rate Monitors" or "Read Our Reviews" would then link to a page that lists individual products sold by that merchant.

Alternatively, the affiliate may prefer to list individual models on the manufacturer's page to expedite delivery of visitors to the exact product they are looking for. Figure 6.3 is an example of this kind of display.

Figure 6.2 Example of Subcategory Page

A **heart rate monitor** is a device that allows a user to measure his or her heart rate in real time. It usually consists of two elements: a chest strap transmitter and a wrist receiver (which usually doubles as a watch). Strapless heart rate monitors are available as well, but lack some of the functionality of the original design. Advanced models additionally measure heart rate variability to assess a user's fitness.

HEART RATE MONITOR MANUFACTURERS

Polar Heart Rate Monitors: A Polar Heart Rate Monitor provides vital information on how your body reacts to physical effort so you can get the most out of your exercise and use your time more efficiently.

Read Our Reviews

Reebok Heart Rate Monitors: Reebok heart rate monitors are ideal for amateur and mature athletes, whose primary aim is to exercise for well-being, weight loss, and/or cardiac rehabilitation. Easy operation and extra large numbers make Reebok heart rate monitors user-friendly.

Read Our Reviews

Timex® Heart Rate Monitors: Timex® Digital Heart Rate Monitors incorporate the latest digital technology from Timex® with fitness methodology used by the fitness experts and personal trainers of the Ironman Institute.

Read Our Reviews

Figure 6.3   Model Listing

Timex Heart Rate Monitors: Timex Digital Heart Rate Monitors incorporate the latest digital technology from Timex with fitness methodology used by the fitness experts and personal trainers of the Ironman Institute.

Models

IRONMAN* TRIATHLON® 100-Lap Digital Heart Rate Monitor

TIMEX Chrono Alarm Timer

1440 Series

Each underlined section of text in the models section would then link to an individual product review page. (How to prepare a product endorsement or review is covered in Chapter 7.)

Comparison Sites

Larger price comparison sites such as BizRate.com and MySimon. com utilize sophisticated software to draw product data and current prices from one or more merchants with whom they are affiliated. These sites offer their visitors the ability to compare prices, benefits, features, and editorial and visitors' reviews of different products side by side. Many of these price comparison sites have their own affiliate programs through which they share revenues paid by their primary merchant partners. For example, LetsTalk.com is a cell phone plan comparison site that has an affiliate program through the Commission Junction affiliate network at CJ.com.

CardOffers.com is a credit card directory that offers information about a large variety of credit card offers from various merchants to online viewers and potential applicants. Its editors maintain all credit card content, such as rates, annual percentage rate (APR), fees, benefits, and term. CardOffers.com also extends credit card reviews through its partnership network, which allows other Web sites to incorporate and customize the CardOffers.com credit card information while earning revenue on their site.

Affiliates who do not have the time or resources required to develop a massive price comparison site of their own may want to send their traffic directly to such a program. The drawback to joining these programs is that commissions are lower than if the affiliate signs up directly for the merchant's affiliate program.

An alternative comparison model for mom-and-pop types of affiliates is to compare just a few products or services on a single page. For example, if your site is about running, you can do a side-by-side comparison of three of the top brand-name heart rate monitors. A very basic suggested structure for a comparison page is laid out in Figure 6.4.

Comparison reviews convert to sales especially well when the affiliate has experience with the product and can express findings using first-person terms, such as, "I found the XYZ heart rate monitor the most comfortable to wear."

Coupon, Discount, Price Drop, and Deal-of-Day Sites

Many online merchants allow their affiliates to pass savings on to their customers via printable coupons, coupon codes, price drop announcements, and deals of the day. Some affiliate sites specialize in publishing

Figure 6.4   Example of Format for Comparison Page

Product Type Compared			
Name	Product 1	Product 2	Product 3
Rank	1	2	3
Product image	■	■	■
Feature 1			
Feature 2			
Feature 3			
Price			
Affiliate link to product	Buy now	Buy now	Buy now
Link to (review below)	More info	More info	More info
Product type reviews			
Product 1	Summary review—200–400 words in length.		
Product 2	Summary review—200–400 words in length.		
Product 3	Summary review—200–400 words in length.		
Summary conclusion			
Relatively short summary of findings above. Include rating and selection criteria.			

Figure 6.5 101Date.com

101Date.com
Internet Dating Made Simple

Home | Dating Services | **Shopping** | Books & Movies | Dating Tips | Singles eScene

November 6, 2006

Dear Single Friend,

Do you want to meet Mr. or Ms. **Right**? A special friend or a sports buddy? Whatever your fancy (or fantasy), I can help you find friends, a lover - maybe even your soulmate!

My name is *Rosalind Gardner*. Since 1998, I've reviewed 100's of good, bad and very ugly Internet dating services, and listed only the **best dating sites** at 101date.com. So, the sooner you start looking, the sooner you'll get connected. Now go ahead and have FUN! :-)

Cheers, *Rosalind*

P.S. Looking for 'spicier' dating services?

Singles eScene
What's new in online dating? Signup NOW and find out! No spam... ever.

Name [   ]

Email [   ]

[Subscribe NOW!]

Dating Categories
- ALL Sites Listed
- 5Star Dating
- Region/Ethnicity
- 40/50+ Seniors
- Specialty Sites
- Disabled Singles
- Ebony & Interracial
- Faith-Based
- Herpes/HPV
- Mail Order Brides
- Matchmaking
- Speed Dating

Other Services
- Fiancee Visas
- LookBetterOnline
- Romance Tours

Shop Specials!

What's HOT in 2006? Find the perfect gift for your favorite online friend.

Start Burning Fat Tonight and look GREAT for the holidays!

Got time? Check out these beautiful Watchcraft Watches.

FREE iPod Mini offer.

101Date.com Visitor Favorites

1. IWantU.com
2. Yahoo! Personals
3. eHarmony
4. FriendFinder
5. CanadianPersonals.net
6. UK Singles Connection
7. Match.com

Dating Tips and Articles
Learn to write effective personal ads. Become aware internet dating pitfalls of and how to avoid them. Enjoy a safe, rich and rewarding experience with online personals. Read our dating tips.

Rosalind's Online Dating Blog
To get the very latest news about Internet dating sites, visit the Blog on our Sister site, Sage-Hearts.com.

only online coupon offers and have, like the comparison sites, become so large that they in turn have established affiliate programs to market their offerings. Once again however, commissions are usually lower when affiliates partner with these larger, or first-tier, affiliate sites. On the other hand, affiliates may partner directly with merchants to access the same products through merchant data feeds and earn higher commissions in the process.

Hybrid Sites

Hybrid sites are Web sites that incorporate more than one of the strategies discussed above. For example, a content publisher may choose not to write her own heart rate monitor reviews, but link instead to a price comparison page on her site through a data feed supplied by GoldenCan.com. This type of site is the simplest for new webmasters to build because it requires the least amount of software, technical knowledge, and time.

Figure 6.5 is an example of a content/product review site. (Visit 101Date.com, an online dating service, to review the entire site.)

PLAN YOUR LAYOUT

Every page on your site is a potential "landing page" for visitors. A *landing page* is the generic term used for the first page of a Web site. While the landing page may be the homepage, it is just as likely to be a content page.

Design a Logo

In order to orient your visitors to their new surroundings on arrival at your site, it is important that each page be consistent in overall design, navigation, and content placement. Every site needs an attractive logo. Whether your logo is your URL produced as a graphic image in a fancy font or a professionally designed logo—your site should sport a unique and attractive logo. A logo sets your site apart and makes it memorable. It will certainly be more memorable than those sites that simply enlarge and make boldface the company's name into a ragged and ugly looking typeface.

Logos are usually positioned in the top left or the top right-hand corner of every page and are linked back to the site's homepage. A professionally designed graphic logo is a great investment in the future of your site. (Two sites that do custom logos are GotLogos. com and TheLogoCreator.com.)

Include a Catchy Slogan

A tag line or slogan quickly helps to define your site's purpose for visitors. Your slogan should be memorable and help visitors to remember your site's name. It should also be short—no more than four or five words in total. Good slogans are original, simple, and believable, and they include a key benefit. Following are a few slogans from both affiliate and merchant sites to get you thinking:

EDiets.com—Your Diet. Your Way.

MakeUpAlley.com—Street Smart Beauty

RoadRunnerSports.com—World's Largest Running Store

Nike—Just Do It

L'Oreal—Because You're Worth It

Wheaties—Breakfast of Champions

101Date.com—Internet Dating Made Simple

Capture Visitors' Names and E-Mail Addresses

Every page should include a form so that you can capture your visitors' names and e-mail addresses. This point is critical. Because visitors will land on pages other than your homepage, place a sign-up form for your opt-in mailing list or newsletter on each and every page of your site.

Develop Consistent Navigation

Your visitors should be able to navigate to any page on your site within three mouse clicks of the homepage. It is really easy to keep your site elements consistent when you use the same template for every page on your site. Essentially, consistency is about making it easy for your visitors to find what they want. That means keeping your navigation, logo, e-zine sign-up form, and all other elements that repeat from page to page in the same place on every page.

Each page should be clearly identified with a headline, and headline fonts should be consistent in color and size from page to page. As readers become accustomed to a consistent site layout, they can move quickly and easily through your site, which makes their experience enjoyable.

Include Your Contact Information

Every page should include a link to your homepage, contact information, and "About Us" page. Including "Home | About Us | Contact Us" as simple text at the bottom of every page is often a good idea and helps keep visitors from getting lost.

In addition to linking back to your homepage from your logo graphic, a simple text link to "home" on every page will help people find their way around your site. Many affiliate marketers neglect to include their contact information for fear that visitors may overwhelm them with e-mail or phone them in the middle of the night. These fears are unwarranted and unrealistic. Simply knowing that they can get in touch with you is often enough to confirm the site's credibility for most visitors. Visitors who do take the time to write are demonstrating their interest in the site's offerings. A timely response will often clinch the deal and make the sale.

Rather than posting clickable e-mail links, you may wish to use a contact form for a couple of reasons. First, forms help eliminate the spammers who use harvesters to collect thousands of e-mail addresses. Second, it can be disconcerting for your visitor when his or her e-mail software opens suddenly when they are expecting to see a form.

It is natural for customers to want to know with whom they are doing business, especially before they pull out their wallets. To build credibility with your customers, create an "About Us" page on your site and include both your picture and your reasons for creating your Web site on that page. When your visitors learn that you created "Ron's Running Site" site because you are a marathon runner and coach, they will have faith in you and the information on your site.

Guarantee Customers' Privacy

Every commercial Web site needs a privacy/security statement. Some affiliate agreements even stipulate that your site must contain a privacy statement. Privacy statements explain how information on your site is collected, safeguarded, and used. It is an explicit statement made on behalf of the site owner to the site user, and it is a legal, binding document. Including a privacy statement instills user confidence and trust, reduces liability, and increases your Web site's conversion rate.

Your site should indicate compliance with the Child Online Privacy Protection Act (COPPA) if needed. If your site is located in the United States, it is definitely needed. (You, however, are responsible for determining needed compliance.) For more complex privacy statements and other forms, visit FindLegalForms.com.

These work to instill credibility with your visitors. Be sure to incorporate elements on your site to improve ease of use for your visitors and improve your conversion rates as well.

Create a Paper Outline First

Building a themed Web site is similar to writing an essay. As you may remember from your school days, the best way to approach an essay is to develop an outline first. An outline helps to organize your thoughts and present the material in a logical manner that will make it easy for your visitors to use and understand your site. If your outline is good, your site content will be easy and quick to write. Take a look at how the site might be ordered logically into categories and individual pages. In the following example, we use the process to lay out a Web site on the subject of running.

Build a Category List from Your Keyword List During the process of researching a niche and finding products to promote, you will have developed a long list of keywords and topics for your site. In Chapter 3, "Market Research," there is a keyword list related to a running site. The keyword list is repeated here, in Figure 6.6.

This list contains generic terms and possible categories as well as product types, names, and manufacturers.

Figure 6.6 Keyword List

10K	races
10k run	racing
5K	REFLECTIVE CLOTHING
5k race	run
5k run	runner
800 metres	runners
ADIDAS RUNNING SHOES	running
AIF	running a marathon
Arkansas running clubs	RUNNING ACCESSORIES
ASICS RUNNING SHOES	running advice
athletics	RUNNING APPAREL
BABY JOGGERS	running apparel
Bass	RUNNING CLOTHES
beginners running	running clothing
BROOKS RUNNING SHOES	running club
brooks running shoes	running clubs
brooks running socks	running events
CD	running exercise
cross country	running fitness
CROSS COUNTRY SHOES	RUNNING JACKET
discount running shoes	RUNNING PANTS
etonic running shoes	RUNNING RACES
event calendar	running shoes
exercise	RUNNING SHORTS

(Continued)

Figure 6.6   (Continued)

field	RUNNING SOCKS
fitness	RUNNING STORES
GAIT ANALYSIS	running technique
HEART RATE MONITORS	SALOMON TRAIL SHOES
HYDRATION SYSTEMS	SAUCONY RUNNING SHOES
London marathon	SUN GLASSES
marathon	track
MIZUNO RUNNING SHOES	TRACK SHOES
NATHAN REFLECTIVE GEAR	TRACK SPIKES
NEW BALANCE RUNNING SHOES	TRAIL SHOES
NIKE RUNNING SHOES	training
PEDOMETERS	Video
POLAR HEART RATE MONITORS	VIDEO GAIT ANALYSIS
race	workouts
race calendar	

Create an Ordered List of Categories You have probably seen sites that list 40 or more items in the navigation bar. This is too many options for most people to scan. You must therefore create an ordered list of first-, second-, and possibly even third-tier categories.

As first-tier categories form your site's primary navigation, try to limit the number of items in your list. For example, from the keyword list in Figure 6.6, you might establish a first-tier category list as follows:

Training

Apparel

Shoes

Gear and gadgets

Nutrition

Motivation

Health

Travel

You will then build a subcategory list for each first-tier category. For example, a subcategory list for gear and gadgets might look like this:

Heart rate monitors

Injury and prevention

Packs and bottles

Pedometers

Safety gear

Strollers

Treadmills

Watches

Note: Arrange second-tier categories alphabetically to help your visitors find what they want quickly.

Most second-tier categories will have to be subcategorized further into third-tier categories. Some will require even further breakdown. Safety gear for example might include reflective garments, headlamps, and reflective or flashing lights.

There are two primary benefits to categorizing your site in this manner. First, naming individual pages according to very specific content can attract free search engine traffic to your site. For example, a page that promotes reflective garments would be named "reflective-garments.html." Both the title within the page and its title "meta tag" should also include the keyword phrase, "Reflective Garments" and "reflective garments," respectively.

Second, good categorization makes it easy for your visitors to find exactly what they are looking for when they are looking through your site. Furthermore, if you use pay-per-click search engines to send traffic to your site, you can send the surfer who typed in the keyword phrase "reflective garments" directly to your "reflective-garments.html" page.

SUPER AFFILIATE TIP

Although planning can become tedious, do not skip the process. The easier you make it for visitors to find exactly what they want, the higher your conversion rates and sales will be.

7

Plan and Develop Content

The average affiliate produces a visitor-to-sales conversion rate of between 0.5 and 1 percent. In other words, they achieve an average conversion rate if they make one sale for every hundred visitors sent to a merchant's site. On the other hand, super affiliates often achieve conversion rates of 2.5 to 6 percent, and sometimes much higher, depending on the type of product sold, when they consistently follow the rules laid out in Chapter 9, "Choose and Join Affiliate Programs."

The real secret to high conversion rates, however, is to give your visitors access to high quantities of great content in various forms. In the following sections, we look at different types of content to use on your site, and the different ways in which you can develop content. Plan to incorporate some or all of the following content elements in your own Web site. If you are not a writer, do not worry about how you will put all this content into your site. In the next section, you will discover how to get content from other sources.

TYPES OF CONTENT

In addition to writing product reviews and endorsements to promote their merchants' products, professional affiliates offer their visitors informative articles, an e-course, and a regular newsletter. Content of an informative nature can be written by either the affiliate or a ghost-writer. In some cases, private label rights packages are available for purchase. We will look at each type of content and ways to produce content in the sections that follow.

Informative Articles

Great content keeps visitors at your Web site for longer than they stay at sites with weak content. It also encourages them to return repeatedly. Links in articles can send visitors directly to your merchants' sites for more information in your product reviews. Well-written, highly relevant articles also help to attract free search engine traffic to your site.

Product Reviews and Endorsements

The best conversion-to-sales ratios are achieved when you write product endorsements and reviews for your merchants' products. If you list a number of similar products, you may want to take a compare and contrast strategy, in addition to providing individual product endorsements. Give the product or service you are promoting added value by creating content around it. Tell your customers exactly why you think it is a good product or service. If it has a few drawbacks, but you still think it is a good buy, tell them that too. It will increase their trust in you.

Give your customers enough information about the product to help them decide whether or not it is right for them, which gives you a big leg up on the competition. Offering extras like informative articles, reports, and newsletters can increase sales and conversion rates. Good sales copy appeals to customers' emotions, not their intellect. Tell them about the benefits they will get from your product or service—how it will make them feel, how it will improve their finances, figure, relationship, whatever. Talk benefits, *not* features.

The best way to promote your merchants' products is to endorse them, in an honest and unbiased manner. In order for your endorsement to be persuasive, you should have personal experience with the product and be enthusiastic about it. Given those two factors, writing the endorsement then becomes easy. That is why super affiliates frequently buy the products they sell. They study the product or service inside and out, backwards and forwards. They note all the features, both good and bad. Writing the recommendation takes time and care. You need to consider carefully all you want to say and anticipate your readers' reactions. If you have doubts about the product or service you want to endorse, either say so or don't write about it at all. Your reputation is at stake.

When you anticipate your visitors' concerns, you are able to address them before they become unanswered questions that cause them to click away. The primary ingredient in a compelling personal testimonial is an explanation of how you benefited from use of the product or service. The product feature list is secondary. People want to know how the product will improve their lives.

Example: If you are promoting the latest health regime, simply emphasizing that the product contains a specific element is unlikely to convince anyone of its worth. Tell your visitors sincerely how it made you feel more fit and energetic and how much more time and energy you had to spend with the kids. That will get them interested. If you want to see examples of product endorsements in action, watch TV infomercials. Infomercial writers are the kings and queens of compelling copy.

E-Course/Autoresponder Series

An *e-course* is a series of informative short articles delivered automatically through an autoresponder service to those who subscribe to a site. An autoresponder is a program that sends automatic replies to people who send e-mails to a particular e-mail address or enter their name and e-mail address into a form on a Web page. There are many autoresponder services available to webmasters. I use and recommend the service provided at http://Aweber.com.

The first message is typically a welcome message that thanks your subscribers for signing up for your newsletter and introduces them to the content they will receive throughout the series.

Using our running site as an example, an autoresponder series might consist of the following messages after the welcome message has been delivered:

- Strength exercises for runners
- How to choose a running shoe
- Avoid injury—stay limber!
- 10 best snacks for runners
- How to stay motivated

- Cold (warm) weather tips for runners
- 10K training tips

Each message within the autoresponder series should be designed to bring visitors back to your site or introduce them to your merchants' products through your affiliate links. For example, in the "strength exercises for runners" message listed on the previous page, you could include a link back to the page on your site that promotes weight sets and barbells. Studies suggest that an autoresponder series should contain no fewer than seven messages; however, some webmasters have a year's worth of messages programmed.

Regular Newsletter

Once visitors sign up to receive your e-course, they are also automatically signed up to receive your regular newsletters. A weekly or biweekly newsletter containing news and information relevant to your site builds rapport and trust with your subscribers and encourages them to revisit your site time and again.

DEVELOP CONTENT

Great content makes for great sites. You can either choose to write your own content if you fancy yourself a bit of a writer, or you can outsource most of your writing and take more time off. So do not worry if you are not a writer. There are five options listed below for content development—in addition to writing your own content:

1. Hire a ghostwriter.
2. Buy resale and private label rights.

   3. Source copyright-free (public domain) work.

   4. Use other writers' content.

   5. Use merchant copy.

Create Your Own Content

If you have always thought of yourself as a writer, now is your chance to prove it. The best thing about writing your own site content is that you can inject your personality. Good Web writers write in a natural, conversational style (unless you are talking about something serious). You are not the CEO of a major corporation; you are a webmaster, so the old-fashioned, cumbersome business style of writing has left the room. It is your site. You can be funny, curmudgeonly, or sweet.

In time, your visitors will start to recognize your "voice." If they like you, they look forward to hearing more of what you have to say. Write as naturally as possible—as if you were writing to your best friend—so your client feels relaxed and happy (or whatever emotion you are trying to evoke). Eventually you build rapport with your readers and develop friendships through your correspondence. That, more than commissions, is what makes this business so sweet.

Hire a Ghostwriter

If you are truly allergic to writing, then you may want to have someone else do the writing for you. Many webmasters build content for their sites quickly and cheaply by using ghostwriters hired through Elance.com and Rentacoder.com.

Do not underpay the ghostwriters you hire. Articles can sell for as little as $2 each, but you get what you pay for, and invariably a $2 article will probably be lackluster and full of grammatical errors. Figure 7.1 is a portion of a very unprofessional ghostwritten article. (Avoid this kind of writing on your site.)

That article was almost certainly written according to a keyword density formula for the terms "cell phone" and "cell phone plans." A keyword density formula specifies repetitive use of chosen keywords and keyword phrases in specific locations throughout an article. Many webmasters who used keyword density formulas in their articles have had their sites deranked and delisted by Google.

To get high-quality articles written by ghostwriters, you need to pay more and be specific about the tone of the article you want.

Figure 7.1 Unprofessional Ghostwritten Article

You are here looking for cell phone family plans, which ones offer the best wireless plans for the money and which have the best free cell phones.

Cell phone family plans that include free cell phones and great cheap wireless plans.

Well try and give you as much information regarding cell phone plans for families as well as finding the best deals on free cell phones and cheap wireless plans.

Whether or not your looking to simply stay in touch with your family easily or your looking to save money on your current wireless plan, family cell phone plans can do that by placing all the cell phones in your family onto one wireless plan. Another great aspect of getting a cell phone family plan is that many wireless plans provide free mobile to mobile minutes so you can stay in touch with you family without running up the bills.

There's no harm in asking for a 100-word example on the topics you want covered. If the writer is a professional and keen to earn both your respect and the project, he or she will be more than happy to oblige in most cases.

Come up with your own review structure and spell out exactly what is required to fulfill your project satisfactorily. Figure 7.2 contains an example of a well-written project description.

Buy Private Label Rights

Private label rights (PLR) and packages with niche content are currently all the rage. PLR are articles and e-books for which you buy the right to use any way you want. Private label rights articles are supplied as unformatted text files or Word documents, to which you can add or modify content, including the title and author's name, meaning that you can put your own name on the article.

PLR packages are quite inexpensive compared to ghostwritten articles. Private label rights articles average 10 to 20 cents apiece, whereas a good ghostwriter will charge between $10 and $30 for one well-written article. You could take a PLR e-book and break it up into individual articles and then use those articles on your site, in your blog, or in your newsletter. Conversely, you might want to combine a number of PLR articles into an e-book to give away as an incentive for people to sign up for your newsletter, or even to sell for a profit. You could even sell your new book on eBay and generate affiliate sales or bring traffic to your site through links in the book.

Consider using the first paragraph or two of each article in your autoresponder series, and include a link to the complete article

Figure 7.2 Project Description

Do You VoIP?

Project description: Do you use VoIP and love the service? If so, we would like you to write articles for us on various topics to inform people about VoIP systems. Here are some examples:

1. *VoIP value proposition*: The top 10 reasons to use VoIP, including details. This will be our lead article.
2. *VoIP reliability*: How technology is today and how VoIP works as well as land lines. Purpose of this article is to remove users' objections.
3. *Buyers guide*: Top 10 things to look for when comparing providers. This should be a comprehensive guide to give the users the confidence and knowledge they need to move forward in the process.
4. *Shoppers guide*: Create a case to switch to VoIP for both homeowners and small businesses.
5. Article that explains the procedure involved to switch from traditional phone services to business VoIP services.
6. Article that states the benefits of VoIP. Describe all VoIP options to help users determine best business VoIP solution for them.
7. Product reviews for top business VoIP providers including ViaTalk, SunRocket, and Vonage.

Each article should be a minimum of 400 words and written in a professional and friendly tone.

No SEO (keyword density formula) writing, please. We want articles that are written by humans for humans.

on your site to bring your visitors back to your site. Before you buy a private label rights package, read the terms of agreement carefully. You want to make sure that you have the right to change, modify, cut, or delete the content in any way you want, as well as put your own name on the work.

Public Domain Works

Public domain works are books, poems, and articles for which the copyright has expired and that have *no* copyright protection. Anyone can copy, modify, and use or sell them. Like PLR articles, you can even remove the original author's name and treat it as your own. Once you modify a public domain work it becomes your property. The modified work receives an automatic copyright just like it would if it were an original work. (See Appendix C, "Recommended Resources," to learn how to source public domain works.)

Use Other Authors' Content

GoArticles.com, EzineArticles.com and a number of other article directories allow you to use the material that authors post to those sites, free of charge. The stipulation is that you respect authors' guidelines and those of the article directory managers. In almost all cases, authors require that you place their resource box at the bottom of the article, which invariably includes a link back to their site. Therein lies the disadvantage to using other authors' material on your Web site.

The link to the author's site will not normally be an affiliate link, and you should rarely post "leaky" or nonpaying links on your site. You are much better off using PLR articles which you can claim as your own and which have no linking requirements.

MERCHANT COPY AND SALES TOOLS

Most merchants provide promotional tools and ad copy that you can place on your site. All you have to do is visit their affiliate interface and then cut and paste their text and banners into your pages. In most cases the links will be coded with your affiliate ID. Please note, however, that using merchant copy—other than basic text links, banner ads, and data feeds—should be an option of *last resort*. Your visitors may have seen a particular merchant's article a number of times already so that when they see it again on your site, they will just click away. For a truly successful site, consider using one of the options listed above before you use merchant copy, such as articles, product reviews, and interviews.

Following are seven different sales tools that merchants may offer their affiliates.

Text Links

Text links are typically formatted in either HTML or javascript and have your affiliate ID encoded directly into the link. The following example is a snippet of HTML code for Yahoo! Personals picked up from Commission Junction affiliate interface. All you need to do is cut and paste the HTML code into your Web page, and your visitors will see the text "Find Romance at Yahoo! Personals."

Example: <a href="http://www.qksrv.net/click-168978-10278403" target="_top">Find Romance at Yahoo! Personals </a><img src="http://www.qksrv.net/image-168978-10278403" width="1" height="1" border="0">

"All-in"Text Links "All-in" text links send your visitors to a landing page on the merchant's site that lists all of the merchants' products. Each product link on that landing page is coded with your affiliate ID number or code, and if any product sale is made, you will earn a commission. Following is an example of an all-in text HTML link for the Friendfinder dating service.

Example: http://seniorfriendfinder.com/go/page/site_directory_ dating.html?pid=g9517

The link sends visitors to a page titled "Top Dating Sites," which lists all of Friendfinders many dating services as seen in Figure 7.3. Your visitors who land on that page can pick the site or category that appeals to them most, and the affiliate will be credited with any sale.

Custom Landing Pages

Friendfinder also provides a number of different custom landing pages to which their affiliates can send traffic. Examples include location, gender, race, and specific pages on the site. Here is an example of a link that is specifically designed to find "Women Seeking Men near Palo Alto, California, between the ages of 18 and 25."

http://friendfinder.com/search/g9517-pct?show=F-M&age= 18-25&geo=Palo Alto,CA

Figure 7.4 shows a partial screen capture of the landing page that shows female members of Friendfinder who are looking for men near Palo Alto, California.

Banners

Banners are graphic images that come in a variety of different sizes. The most popular sizes are 468 × 60 pixels, 125 × 125, 234 × 60, 120 × 60, 120 × 90, and 88 × 31. "Skyscrapers" are generally 120 × 600,

Figure 7.3 Friendfinder All-in Affiliate Link Landing Page

Top Ranking Dating Sites

Category	Dating Sites	Members	Rating
Singles Dating Sites			
	Friendfinder Discover great singles near you. Dating, friendships, relationships, and pen pals.	3 million	★★★★★
	SeniorFriendfinder.com Dating for people with experience. It is never too late to fall in love. You'll find romance, friendships, relationships, pen pals, and more.	430,000	★★★
Adult / Sex / Singles Personals Sites			
	AdultFriendfinder.com The world's largest sex and swingers site connects you to more than 20 million active members. Find adult fun, dating, sex, free personal ads, swingers, swappers, bisexual singles, and more.	20 million	★★★★★
	Alt.com With almost three million active members, ALT.com isn't just the world's largest BDSM & alternative lifestyle personals site, it's an online community. Fetish, fantasy, kink, bondage, domination … find it here.	2 million	★★★★★
	OutPersonals.com Meet real men on the web from our million-plus active membership. Gay singles and couples looking for hookups, dates, and relationships.	1 million	★★★★★

which is the average window height of a computer display. Some companies have half-page banners that are about 480 × 480 pixels in size. Others offer full-page ads with numerous graphics and text and come in a zipped file that you extract to a file on your computer. Figure 7.5 is an example of a banner ad for Shoes.com, sized 468 pixels wide by 60 pixels high.

Interstitial (Pop-Up) Banners An *interstitial banner* ad is an advertisement that appears in a separate pop-up browser window while the main page is still loading, forcing exposure to the advertisement before visitors can see the main content. Be careful if you

Figure 7.4   Friendfinder Geotargetted Landing Page

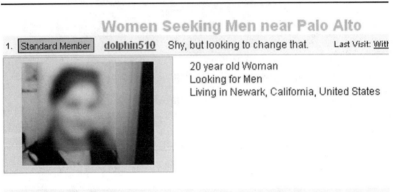

choose to use this type of advertising. While the response rates may be higher, many Internet users have installed "pop-up killers" on their computers, so they will never see your ad. They also may not be able to move forward within your site if they use pop-up-stopping software.

Because pop-ups interrupt the surfing flow, they also breed resentment. About.com was once notorious for its extremely annoying use of interstitials. Although it appears that this site has ceased its use of interstitial inessentials, About.com still uses pop-ups far too frequently.

Figure 7.5 Shoes.com 468- by 60-Pixel Banner

Product Reviews

Not many merchants provide their affiliates with full-scale product reviews, which is a wise move, as overuse of the same articles and product reviews detracts from both the merchant's and the affiliate's reputation. Therefore, limit use of merchants' reviews as guidelines for writing your own product reviews and articles. Furthermore, be sure that the merchant copy you select refers to products that are currently available.

E-Mail Promotions

Sending a promotional e-mail that your merchant writes is easier than creating a page for your site with banners and text. Smart merchants write their own "advertorials" and format them both in HTML and in plain text for affiliates to distribute via e-mail. Because they recognize that hundreds of other affiliates will be using the same material, smart affiliates customize merchants' e-mail promotions to personalize it for their audience.

Interviews

Very few merchants use interviewing; however, it can work brilliantly when used effectively. Affiliates are granted permission to publish interviews that the merchant marketers have given. Interviews tend to have excellent conversion rates because it appears that the reader gets more information than through typical product advertising. Think of the infomercials that you have seen in which the creator of some miracle gel extols its benefits in response to an interviewer's questions. Merchant interviews use the same principle to promote products.

Product Data Feeds

Building an affiliate Web site that sells between five and twenty products is relatively quick and easy to accomplish. An experienced webmaster can easily build a review site that promotes about ten products in a day. An affiliate with less experience might spend a week signing up for the programs, designing a template, and inputting the product information and affiliate links. Spending a week or even a month on a site that delivers big rewards over the years is a relatively minor investment of time.

But how much time and effort is invested by affiliates who promote thousands of items like magazines, garden products, posters, T-shirts, or lingerie? How difficult would it be to place tens of thousands of links to music CDs, or movie DVDs on your site? By using product data feeds, affiliates can build a 500-item site in less than an hour. They can even build a 10,000-item site in less than an hour! A merchant data feed lists names, descriptions, SKU numbers, prices, and other relevant product data.

Data feeds help affiliates increase their conversion rates by getting the customers directly to the product they were looking for and sooner. Customers are supplied with all the information they need to make a buying decision right on the affiliate's site. Then all the merchant needs to do is close the sale. Some merchant data feeds are static and are delivered to the affiliate in a spreadsheet. Affiliates must then process these static data feeds through software, such as WebMerge, available at FourthWorld.com. WebMerge generates static Web pages from your database content. The software works with any database or spreadsheet that exports in tab-delimited or other tabular format. WebMerge creates an HTML page from the data for each record in the spreadsheet and will work with templates that the affiliate supplies. Pages can then be uploaded on any Web server without the need for a specialized database hosting solution.

However, as some merchants amend their product listings daily or even more often, updating pages frequently to stay current can become quite cumbersome. To help affiliates publish the latest information about their products, many merchants now supply their affiliates with dynamic data feeds, which are updated on the affiliate's site without the affiliate having to change anything. Pricing changes and new coupons are reflected in real time on the affiliate site when feeds are dynamic and are hosted by the merchant.

Because dynamic data feeds usually require that affiliates have some programming knowledge and many merchants do not have time to instruct their affiliates on how to install these feeds, third-party companies have stepped in to help both merchants and affiliates get their dynamic feeds up and running. GoldenCan.com has become a leading provider of dynamic feeds to affiliates through its data feed/store integration program. Affiliates may display thousands of merchant products and/or coupons by pasting only a single line of code into their Web pages.

The simplicity of this technology has opened up affiliate marketing opportunities to people who might otherwise be excluded from this type of advanced technology because of their lack of technical skill. Affiliates are supplied with data feeds, coupons, recent price drops, and product searches from hundreds of merchants in one simple line of code.

SUPER AFFILIATE TIP

To save time and make more sales, look for merchants with product data feeds.

8

Build Your Site

Building your Web site can be a quick, cheap, and simple process. It can also be time-consuming, very expensive, and frustrating. It all depends on how much time, money, and energy you are willing to spend and how much you already know. From doing it all yourself to having it all done for you, each option has advantages and disadvantages you should consider.

WAYS TO BUILD A SITE

There are four basic Web site building options: build it yourself, buy a ready-made template, use an e-commerce package, or hire a designer. Determine which one fits your needs and expectations.

Build It Yourself

Building your own Web site is usually the least expensive option, depending on the knowledge you already have about site building. On the other hand, the cost of designing and building your own site can become fairly hefty if you buy the most expensive graphic design programs and HTML editors. It can also be the most time-consuming way to build a site when you are new to the game. However, once you learn a little HTML and have one or two pages under your belt, you will find that knocking pages off takes just a matter of minutes. If you plan to build your own site, following are some software options you might want to consider.

Graphics Software To manipulate or create graphics for your site, you will require image editing that is designed specifically for capturing, creating, and editing images. Examples of these programs include Adobe Photoshop, Jasc Paint Shop Pro, and CorelDRAW.

Jasc Paint Shop Pro (http://www.jasc.com) incorporates nearly all the same features as Adobe Photo Shop but at a fraction of the cost. Paint Shop Pro is easy to use and is a much lighter program to load and run, which is critical because you will often need to have your HTML editor, FTP program, several browser windows, and Paint Shop Pro open all at the same time while building your site.

HTML Editors An HTML editor is a software program that simplifies the creation of HTML Web pages. The two most popular HTML editors used by affiliate marketers are:

- *Adobe's Dreamweaver 8* (*http://www.macromedia.com/soft ware/homesite*): Dreamweaver 8 is a leading Web development tool that enables users to efficiently design, develop, and maintain standards-based Web sites. Its features list is exhaustive.

- *XsitePro (http://xsitepro.com)*: This is quickly becoming the standard HTML editor for use by affiliate marketers because it incorporates many standard features and tools that affiliates want and need such as easy Adsense and article integration.

Buy a Ready-Made Template

The attractiveness, quality, and value of Web site templates currently available are outstanding. Here are three recommended template sites:

- 4Templates.com
- BoxedArt.com
- DollarTemplates.com

Of the three, BoxedArt.com offers the most attractive templates; however, they may be too complex for anyone without some knowledge of HMTL coding. For a very small additional fee, most template designers will make changes to their designs or add information according to your instructions.

Site-Building E-Commerce Package Deals

One option that eliminates the need to learn HTML and incorporates all the features used by affiliates is Site Build It!, also known as SBI!. In addition to site-building templates, the package also includes extensive training in how to build and manage an effective Internet marketing business. Although the initial price may seem rather steep, price comparisons show that you could not buy all the components you need for an Internet business site separately for the price of SBI! Its value increases in the second year when the price goes down.

Even if you could arrange domain registration, Web hosting, autoresponders, HTML editors, and so on for only $25 or $30 per month, you would not enjoy the benefits of accessing all those utilities through a single interface. Site Build It! is proud of its reputation for providing a community-based atmosphere in which the owner, Ken Evoy, is as enthusiastic and committed to your success as you are. The SBI! forum is one of the most helpful and supportive forums you will find on the Net. Whether you have a problem that needs solving, require information on how to make your business grow and prosper, or even if you just want to chat, the SBI! forum is the place to go. The Site Build It! Web site is http://webvista.sitesell.com.

Hire a Designer

Two sites at which you can find Web designers are Elance.com and RentaCoder.com. At both sites, you post a description of your project, and then designers bid on it. If you are going to use a Web designer, be sure that he or she understands what you want to achieve with your affiliate Web site. As an example, many Web designers use lots of flash elements, which the search engines ignore. Such elements take up heaps of bandwidth and are really there only to make your site look pretty. It is best to avoid such flashy elements.

Your project description should include the type of theme and tone you want for your site. If you have seen similar sites that contain certain elements you like, mention them in your project description. Be sure to let the designer know that you wish to design an affiliate Web site, and then look for a designer whose portfolio includes affiliate sites.

Be clear about your site's objective; include what you would like to see on each page, clear and precise instructions about navigational links, and how many pages the site will have in total. Study the basic design rules Super Affiliates use that are described in the next section, and apply them to your project details. Be wary of graphic designers and artists whose key objective is to produce a work of art. You are not looking for a masterpiece; you want a fully operational, clean, and bug-free Web site that addresses all your needs.

Finally, remember that when the project is completed, you want total control over its use, so the Web site and all its code should be available to you so that you can make the necessary changes you will need to make over the lifetime of your Web site.

Regardless of which option you choose to build your site, I highly recommend that you make time to learn *some* basic HTML coding. Waiting for someone else to make changes to your site can be frustrating and costly. It is much better for you to maintain control over all aspects of your affiliate business.

GUIDELINES FOR GOOD WEB SITE DESIGN

While it is not within the scope of this book to give detailed instruction on Web design, here are some basic design rules that Super Affiliates generally follow.

Fonts

You may love the appearance of an unusual font; however, there are a couple of problems with using fonts that are not common to everyone's computer. If the font you use on your site is not resident on your visitor's computer, your text will not appear as intended. The second problem with unique or frilly fonts is legibility. Script and unusual fonts should be used sparingly and rendered in a larger size so that they are readable to all your visitors. The standard and best fonts for use on the web are arial, verdana, and tahoma.

Text should be large enough to read without surfers having to adjust their browser's font size display—because most visitors will not go to the trouble. They will visit another site to find the information they want—one that does not make them squint. In addition, text should always be dark on a light background. Although white text on black may look attractive, it is difficult to read, and you will find that visitors will eventually give up before they have finished reading your product reviews. Once again, the result is fewer conversions to sales.

Links

Use standard linking practices to avoid confusion. If visitors are unable to distinguish links from regular text, they are not going to click your links. Standard link colors are:

Underlined blue: unvisited link
Red: active link or "hover"
Purple: visited link

Changing the link or font colors is quick and easy when you use CSS, or cascading style sheets. CSS eliminates the need to code the font face, size, and color every time you wish to make a change to a word's appearance. Instead, each font specification is contained in a single CSS file, and all pages that link to the style sheet share the same font attributes. By eliminating font coding by using CSS, the size of your pages is reduced. You will find hundreds of CSS tutorials by simply searching Google.com for "CSS." HTMLGoodies.com is a great place to start learning the basics.

Color Schemes

Different colors have different meanings and connotations, and some color combinations are just plain ugly. A health and fitness site probably would not thrive with a sickly combination of lavender and olive green as well as it would with vibrant colors. A financial site would surely be doomed if all its visitors saw was red. Think about what your site's colors convey, and use those that complement the theme.

White Space

White space, or negative space, describes open space between design elements. White space is an important layout technique often over-looked by inexperienced designers. Visually appealing design is easy on the eyes. Without adequate white space, text would be unreadable, graphics would lose their emphasis, and there would be no balance between the elements on a page.

White space takes on added importance in Web sites because the more there is to read, the more eyestrain we experience when reading printed material. White space gives our eyes and our brains a break. Treat white space as more than just a background. Treat it as an integral part of your page design.

Page Width

Forcing your visitors to scroll right in order to see all the text on a page is a symptom of poor design or a lack of knowledge of standard display sizes. Standard screen resolutions are 1024 by 768 pixels, for those with good eyesight. However, many, many folks still use 800 by 600. Design for the lowest common denominator of screen size, which is 800 pixels wide by 600 pixels tall. That means that the 800-, 1024-, 1152-, *and* the 1280-pixel wide people can all see the whole page on their display.

You can also use percentage widths, that is, use the HTML code width = "100 percent," which widens or narrows the page according to each surfer's screen resolution. However, your pages will appear differently on different computer displays and in different browsers when you use this coding technique. It is better to design your pages so that they are consistent across various platforms and hard-code specific widths for your HTML pages.

Page Backgrounds

It is simply astounding to see how many Web builders think that their visitors will waste time squinting to read text on a floral, striped, or otherwise busy background. You will probably get a headache just looking at the background depicted in Figure 8.1. Imagine if you had to read a portion of text with that image in the background.

Audio

Have you ever clicked to a Web site and had your eardrums immediately assaulted by loud music? Or how do you like those pages that open with a voice-over monologue? Under no circumstance should a site broadcast noise and/or music without the visitor's permission. Even if a site is about music, visitors should have the option to listen to what they want to hear and when they want to hear it. That is just basic courtesy.

Figure 8.1   Inappropriate "I Think It's Ugly or Unattractive"
Web Site Background

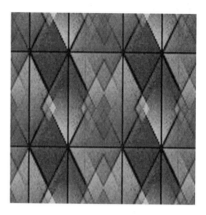

Music or noise that has your visitor clutching at her heart in fear will only hurt you because she may caution others against visiting your site. Consider the possibility that your visitors may be in an office or library environment while quietly surfing the Net. Any sudden unexpected noise will disrupt what they are doing, and they are likely to retreat from your site in great haste. However, audio is perfectly acceptable when the visitor can click a link to listen to the recording. Hearing a real person talk about your product can also increase your conversion rates substantially. If you want to create an audio message, the best software for audio recording is Jay Jennings' "Sonic Memo" available at SonicMemo.com.

Fast-Loading Pages

Every time characters of information are downloaded from, or uploaded to, a Web site, bandwidth is used. As more bandwidth is used, data and information transmission times increase. Surfers have short attention spans, and most still do not have cable or fast ADSL connections. Therefore, page elements that slow down the time it takes to display your Web pages may be reducing your income as impatient surfers click their "back" buttons.

Site elements that hog bandwidth include large or animated graphics, Flash, and audio elements of any kind. If you need graphics on your pages, compress them to the smallest size that does not affect their appearance.

Pop-Ups

Web surfers do not like pop-up windows, and many have installed pop-up blockers on their browsers. Focus on your customers, and limit the use of pop-ups as much as possible.

Frames

Frames have one main page, and several secondary pages. This feature saves the Web developer from having to add navigation to every page on the site. What it does not do, however, is allow you to link to individual pages and have your site design or layout appear on the framed page. Visitors cannot link to specific pages on your site if the pages are within a frame. The URL that appears in their browser's address bar remains the same the entire time they navigate your site. So if they choose to bookmark a page, they are actually bookmarking the homepage, not the page they wanted to bookmark. Search engine robots have a hard time spidering sites that are built in frames. Although there are ways to optimize your framed site to be attractive to search engines, the reasons above should negate any compulsion you feel to use frames.

CHECK YOUR SITE IN DIFFERENT BROWSERS

Install multiple browsers on your computer to see how your Web pages render or look in each browser. Although less than 10 percent of surfers use Netscape to surf the Net, 10 percent of your advertising budget is a lot of money to throw out the window if your visitors cannot see your pages as they were intended. Following are a few browsers you can investigate.

- *Microsoft's Internet Explorer* (*http://www.microsoft.com/windows/ie/default.asp*).   The most popular browser. Recent reports show that 90 to 95 percent of Web surfers access the Internet with IE (Internet Explorer).

- *Netscape Communicator/Navigator* (*http://channels.netscape.com/ns/browsers/download.jsp*).   Another browser currently being used on the World Wide Web, made by Netscape Communications.

- *Mozilla Firefox (http://www.mozilla.org/products/firefox/)*. A popular browser used by millions, particularly for its privacy and security features.

MAKE YOUR PAGES SEARCH ENGINE FRIENDLY

Every webmaster wants his or her site to rank well within search engine results. Following are some tips that will help your pages obtain good rankings and placement.

Build Keyword-Rich Pages

Imagine that one of the pages you have planned for your site is about training Labrador retriever puppies. "Training Labrador Puppies" could then be the main keyword phrase for that page. Use the phrase throughout the text on that page in a way that is natural for people to read.

Keyword stuffing, or overuse of a particular phrase on a page, can result in your page, or your site, being deranked or even delisted from the search engine results.

Use Relevant Content

Jill Whalen, a well-known search engine expert, advises that you work with at least 250 words on a page for the purpose of search engine optimization. Placing more or fewer words will also work, but Jill makes the point that you need at least 250 words to be able to repeat your keyword phrases a number of times throughout the page without seeming dopey.

Name Pages According to Page Content

Name your pages using keywords that are relevant to the product sold on that page or to the most relevant content. For example, a page about training Labrador puppies should be named training-labrador-puppies.html to achieve the best search engine ranking results.

Create a Site Map

Your site should have a site map with links that point to all the important pages and sections. If your site consists of 100 or more pages, break the site map into separate pages. Once the search engine spiders locate your site map, the door is open for them to find all the pages on your Web site and rank them accordingly.

Order Pages

Search engines do not read graphics or javascript, and they get confused when they encounter nested tables. If graphics and javascript precede the first most important keyword phrases on your page, your ranking may be lowered because the search engine considers that phrase less relevant due to its low placement on the page.

Search engine spiders prefer HTML text, loaded with keywords, placed high on the page, and the left side is read before the right side. Therefore, place your primary navigation on the right side of your pages so that the spiders can get to their "food" more quickly.

Include Meta Tags

Meta tags should be included on each page. *Meta tags* provide such information as the author, date of creation and updates for the page, and keywords that indicate the subject matter. Search engines often use keywords included in meta tags to index their databases. The two meta tags that you need to be most concerned about are the title and description tags. Following is a discussion of these and others:

- *Title tag.* The title tag is perhaps one of the most crucial factors in how a search engine will rank your site. The text you use in the title tag must include the most relevant keyword phrases. The title tag must also make sense because it contains the wording that appears on the reverse bar of your browser. That is the blue bar right across the top of your browser window. Title tag text is also the text that most of the search engines will display as the title for your search engine listings.

- *Description tag.* Some search engines use the text contained in your meta description tag as your listing description. Meta description tags also influence your site's ranking in the engines, so you should repeat your primary keyword phrase once or twice in the description, perhaps dropping in a secondary keyword for good measure.

- *Keyword tags.* There was a time when webmasters stuffed keyword meta tags with every keyword relevant to their site—and then they added some more. Most search engine experts now advise that the keyword meta tag is no longer valuable, and apparently only Inktomi and Teoma now index sites using the keyword meta tag. Following are examples of how you would structure the meta tags for a page that reviewed treadmills.

  <title> Treadmill Reviews, Ratings and Buying Tips</title>

  <meta name="description" CONTENT="Read our unbiased treadmill reviews and buying tips so you can choose the treadmill that suits you best.">

  <meta name="keywords" CONTENT="treadmills, buying tips, reviews">

- *ALT tags.* The ALT tag, which stands for "alternative text," is primarily used when images are not shown in the visitor's browser window. ALT tags were originally intended to make a site more accessible to people who are visually impaired and use text readers. However, to boost keyword frequency and achieve better site rankings, many webmasters enter keyword phrases relevant to the page, such as:

  <img src="gifs/logo.gif" width="309" height="97" alt="Treadmill Reviews">

Link Dynamic Pages

Dynamic pages, which deliver content based on user input or other variables, can be more useful and responsive to visitor needs than regular static HTML pages. However, when indexing your site, if a search engine encounters a dynamically generated page—as distinguished by a question mark (?) in the URL—the search engine stops indexing the site at that point.

The simplest method to get dynamic pages indexed is to link to them from a static page, preferably a site map. Although search engines cannot index the whole page, they will index the majority of a page's content. Other solutions involve software and scripting fixes that let search engines index their dynamic content. To learn more about these reconfigurations and rewrites, please consult your usual sources of information on specific programming language.

Avoid Using "Tricks"

Google makes site quality recommendations similar to those below to help you avoid having your site removed from its index. Once a site has been removed, it will not show up on Google.com or on Google's partner sites. The same suggestions hold true for all the major engines.

Do not deceive your users by presenting content to search engines that is different from what is displayed on your pages. A common trick in the past was to include highly popular but irrelevant keywords in meta tags to get "the click." While that brought traffic to the site, the visitor was disappointed by results that had nothing to do with their search, and the engines appeared not to be able to produce relevant results. The search engines now pay attention to such tactics and will remove those using deceptive practices from their index.

Also avoid tricks intended to improve search engine rankings. These include using hidden text or links, sneaky redirects, pages loaded with irrelevant keywords, and the use of "doorway" pages. A *doorway page* is a page made specifically to rank well in search engines. Google also recommends against creating subdomains and domains with essentially duplicate content.

Following these guidelines will help the search engines find, index, and rank your site, which is the best way to ensure that you will be included in the their results. Concentrate your energy on giving your visitors a good experience, rather than on trying to manipulate the search engines. You will be rewarded with traffic and sales, and you will also sleep better at night than your deceptive webmaster counterparts—the so-called black hats.

WEB SITE BUILDING RESOURCES

Following are four excellent resources for those who want to learn more about building a great Web site.

- *HTML Goodies.* Ignore the name. HTMLGoodies.com may have started the site with just HTML tutorials, but now it offers primers in ASP, CGI, CSS, javascript, and Perl to name just a few. It is the very best recommendation for anyone wanting to learn how to build his or her own Web site.

   http://www.htmlgoodies.com/primers/basics.html

- *Hex and Word Colors Codes.* "Aquamarine and dark olive green should never together be seen. YUK!" The colors *and* some poetry! Visit the color code chart to find colors that complement each other.

   http://webmonkey.wired.com/webmonkey/reference/color_codes

- *WebDeveloper.com Forums.*   This is the site you visit when you have a programming question for which your kids do not have the answer.

  http://forums.webdeveloper.com

- *Web Pages That Suck.*   Vincent Flanders's site Web Pages That Suck is where you learn good Web design by looking at bad Web design. With an incredibly fine sense of humor, Mr. Flanders demonstrates by example all the evils of bad Web design. It is a fun way to learn!

  http://webpagesthatsuck.com

9

Choose and Join
Affiliate Programs

Many new Internet marketers confuse the terms *affiliate* and *reseller*, while others confuse multilevel marketing (MLM) with affiliate marketing. To set the record straight, we compare each of those marketing methods in this chapter.

AFFILIATE PROGRAMS VERSUS MLM AND RESELLING

It does not cost anything to join affiliate programs, whereas resellers must buy the products they sell. Multilevel marketers usually must buy sufficient quantities of the products they market to qualify for earnings at a certain tier or level.

Affiliates typically earn a percentage of the purchase price, whereas resellers retain 100 percent of the proceeds of product sales. Some affiliate programs offer webmasters the opportunity to earn a percentage in the second tier by paying a fee for each new affiliate that joins via their program, while some others pay a percentage of their second-tier affiliates' earnings. Other programs pay in both situations. Although this structure is similar to MLM, affiliate marketers are not required to purchase products to be eligible to build their affiliate downline (affiliates that they refer to the program and from whom they will earn a percentage of commissions when that second-tier affiliate makes a sale or generates a lead as per the program terms).

Resellers and many multilevel marketers must handle their own product fulfillment, including carrying inventory, order processing, and shipping. In the case of affiliate marketing, the merchant handles all of these responsibilities. Each affiliate sells the product for the same price. Resellers can often set their own prices, although competitors may undermine their efforts by offering the same product for a lower price.

Although affiliates can collect names and e-mail addresses from visitors to their sites, the affiliates rarely know exactly who buys their affiliated merchants' products. Because resellers handle product fulfillment themselves, they collect names and e-mail addresses from those who buy their products, in addition to those who sign up for the opt-in lists on their sites. This benefits the resellers in that they can do follow up or back-end sales to existing customers.

As with any opportunity, there are advantages and disadvantages to both affiliate marketing and reselling, and both methods can yield decent profits. Although this book deals only with affiliate marketing, you may wish to consider buying resale rights for products relevant to your site when you have gained experience as an affiliate and are ready to expand your online marketing horizons.

AFFILIATE PROGRAM CONSIDERATIONS

There are a number of factors to consider before you join any affiliate program. Items you should consider before affiliating with most merchants are discussed below.

Work with Reputable Companies

Most merchants are reputable operators. However, just because someone has a Web site does not mean that the business is legitimate or that this person is trustworthy. Doing your homework first may save you hundreds, perhaps even thousands, of dollars.

Commission Junction posts the date that merchants join its affiliate network. You can feel reasonably confident when you see that a merchant has been associated with Commission Junction for a year or more—it is in business to do business. Furthermore, some networks require merchants to have funds on deposit to ensure that affiliates are paid what they are owed. You can also search Yahoo! Search Marketing to see how many sponsored listings there are for a specific product and company. If there is more than one listing, the rest of the sites are probably affiliate sites. However, if only one listing is returned, the company may not permit affiliates to advertise its trademarked name.

Search Google for the site name. For example, if you want to promote the Web host HostRocket, do a search at Google for "HostRocket." Are thousands of results returned? Good! Now visit a number of sites that showed up in the regular listings. Read the reviews and check for affiliate links on the site. Are the reviews positive and enthusiastic? You can also contact the webmaster of one of those sites and ask about his or her experience with the program.

Read the Affiliate Agreement

Most affiliate programs have contracts, or affiliate agreements, in place. Before joining, affiliates must indicate their acceptance of the terms of agreement. Affiliate agreements are usually lengthy and peppered with long-winded legalese. Do not let that deter you from reading the agreement completely and carefully, or you could be in for an unpleasant surprise. If the program you are considering does not have an agreement published on the site, find another program to join.

Some affiliate programs stipulate eligibility requirements in their agreements. Pay particular attention to criteria that have been set for acceptance into an affiliate program. Figure 9.1 shows a sample affiliate agreement.

On occasion, your site may meet all the criteria, but your application may be rejected. If you still wish to join the program, e-mail the program manager to state your case and ask that your site be reconsidered for inclusion in their program.

Exclusivity An exclusivity clause is one that stipulates that if you promote that merchant's products, you may not partner with other merchants selling similar products. Keep your options open and refrain from joining programs that require your site to sell one merchant's products exclusively.

Termination Clause In most cases, either the affiliate or the company may choose to cancel an agreement at any time without written notice of cancellation. Make sure that this is what happened, however. Getting out of a contract is usually much more difficult and costly than getting into one. Avoid companies that require signed agreements. There are plenty of programs that are happy to have

Figure 9.1 Sample Affiliate Agreement

Site Requirements

Sites must be hosted on a top-level domain and have a minimum of 2,000 unique visitors per day. Exceptions may be considered for sites that offer substantial and qualified content or that appeal to a sniche targeted audience.

Sites must be professionally designed and contain substantial content.

We accept site applications only from the United States and Canada. Exceptions will be considered for sites whose traffic consists of 90 percent U.S. residents.

Sites must be in English.

Sites must not contain content or links to pornography, hate, or any illegal content.

Sites with e-mail newsletters must adhere to CAN-SPAM. (The CAN-SPAM [Controlling the Assault of Non-Solicited Pornography and Marketing] Act establishes requirements for those who send commercial e-mail, spells out penalties for spammers and companies whose products are advertised in spam if they violate the law, and gives consumers the right to ask e-mailers to stop spamming them. More info can be found at http://www.ftc.gov/bcp/conline/pubs/buspubs/canspam.htm.)

Any attempts at fraud will result in nonpayment and suspension of your account. Falsifying information in your account constitutes expulsion from the network.

The company reserves the right to refuse any site for any reason.

you join without strings. Read and understand the affiliate agreement thoroughly. If you do not understand a clause, ask questions. The merchant's response may not seem fair or make sense, but at least you will have done your homework.

Program Fees

Ninety-nine point nine percent of merchants do not charge a fee to join their affiliate programs. If they do, it is an MLM (multilevel marketing) plan. Six Figure Income (SFI) is an example of an MLM plan that refers to itself as an affiliate program. In order to earn income with SFI, you must purchase some of the company's products each and every month to qualify for sales earnings that you have generated within a month.

Commission Structure and Rates

You must understand commission structures and compare payout rates between affiliate programs. This will affect to what extent you promote individual products. There are essentially three types of affiliate programs: pay-per-sale, pay-per-lead, and pay-per-click:

- *Pay-per-sale programs* are also known as *partnership and percentage partners programs*. These programs pay either a fixed dollar amount or a percentage of sales generated by your links.
- With *pay-per-lead programs*, you earn a set amount whenever your customer fills out a survey or requests a quote or some other kind of information.
- *Pay-per-click programs* are similar to pay-per-lead programs. Essentially you are paid each time one of your visitors clicks on the link through to that program's site.

The Commission Rate Figure 9.2 shows a partial screen shot of merchants returned by the Commission Junction interface for a search for running shoes.

There is a vast difference between commission structures and payout amounts offered by the merchants represented in the figure— anywhere from a low of 6 percent to a high of 20 percent. As a rough guideline, look first for companies that pay the highest per-sale and per-lead commissions in your category of interest. Once you have established a short list, then you can start weeding out those merchants that do not make your cut.

Recurring Commissions If you plan to promote a product that people sign up to buy month after month, such as hosting services or membership sites, make sure the merchant offers recurring commissions. A program that offers residual commissions pays you every time the customer renews the subscription to a specific product.

Let's say that you send Mr. Samson to Best Host Company, and he signs up for the deluxe Web server package at $200 per month. If Best Host Company's affiliate program pays 50 percent commissions only on the initial sale, you will earn $100 total. However, let's say that the program pays 50 percent commissions on the initial sale and 10 percent recurring commissions for every month the subscriber continues to host his site with the service. If Mr. Samson remains a member for five years, you would earn $100 for the first month and $20 for each of the remaining 59 months, for a total of $1,280. If you have a choice between programs, the best option is that one that offers recurring or residual commissions.

On the other hand, a program that pays lifetime commissions pays the affiliate a commission for each and every product that the customer buys from that merchant, including residual commissions,

Figure 9.2   Commission Rate Comparison

Results 1 - 9 of 9			
☑ Apply to Program Select All			
Advertiser	Sale	Lead	Click
☐ **shoes**.com Shoes.com » View Links » View Products	Sale: 17.50% - 20.00% USD		
☐ Activa Sports » View Links	Sale: 8.00% USD		
☐ altrec.com Altrec.com Outdoors » View Links » View Products	Sale: 6.00% USD Performance Incentive		
☐ Zappos.com Zappos.com » View Links » View Products	Sale: 15.00% USD Performance Incentive		
☐ Famous Footwear Famous Footwear » View Links » View Products	Sale: 15.00% USD		
☐ DesignerShoes.com » View Links » View Products	Sale: 13.00% USD Performance Incentive		

if applicable. For example, let's say that you are still earning recurring commissions on Mr. Samson's Web hosting subscription at Best Host Company.

If the company does not offer lifetime commissions and Mr. Samson upgrades his deluxe package to a super deluxe package, you will not get paid commissions on his new order because it is a different product. If Best Host Company offers lifetime commissions, however, the customer you refer to the company is "yours" for life, regardless of which products he or she buys.

Joining programs that offer residual or lifetime commissions is an excellent way to build a steadily increasing income. Once you make a referral, the checks keep coming in. So even when you take a vacation from your affiliate business, the checks for your residuals will also keep coming in.

Two-Tier Programs A *two-tier program* is one that offers two sources of income, the first for bringing in business and the second for recommending new affiliates. Some programs pay a fee for each new affiliate that joins the program, while others pay a percentage of the second-tier affiliate's earnings. Other programs pay in both situations.

When the subject of two-tier programs comes up, the question often arises as to whether two-tier affiliate programs are MLM (multilevel marketing) plans. Also known as network marketing, MLM is essentially any business in which compensation occurs at two or more levels. For example, a company that pays you for the sales you make and also pays you a percentage of the sales made by those you have recruited as sellers is an MLM company.

According to that definition, two-tier affiliate programs are MLM programs. Does it matter? Should it matter? Do not let the MLM association scare you or put you off. There are many reputable MLM organizations including Avon, Mary Kay Cosmetics, and PartyLite Gifts, Inc. MLM has gotten a bad reputation from companies that focus only on recruiting new members and downline-building (recruiting other members). Essentially the only products these companies sell are memberships, which you must purchase in order to be eligible to build your own downline of members.

Your primary concern is whether the company you sign up with is selling real goods and/or services that benefit its customers. Focus first on marketing the product and second on recruiting affiliates. That is why the program is called two tier.

Cookies You may have heard that it takes seven exposures to a product before people feel comfortable enough to buy that product. So what happens if a visitor from your site clicks through to your affiliated merchant site today but does not buy anything until a week later? Will you still get credit for the sale?

That depends on the duration of the cookie. A *cookie* is a coded piece of information, stored on a computer, which identifies that computer during the current and subsequent visits to a Web site. Cookies are coded to expire after a set amount of time. So if the merchant gives cookies that last for 90 days, you get credit if a visitor from your site returns to the merchant and makes the purchase within 90 days. If your visitor purchases the product after the 90 days and the cookie has expired, you are out of luck. You will not get credit for the sale. For example, if Bank #1 sets 30-day cookies for its credit card promotion, while Bank #2's cookies are set to last for only 1 day, you would be crazy to promote Bank #2's credit card when it is a clear-cut example of a merchant taking advantage of its affiliates.

Questions about Payments

Are My Sales Statistics Reported in Real Time? Can you imagine waiting a month to find out if you made a sale for a particular program? Suppose you were spending money to advertise a program, and it took a month to assess the success of your promotional efforts. Would you join that program? No? Good!

When you sign up for an affiliate program, be sure that it offers real-time sales tracking, or something fairly close to real time. *Real time* actually means immediate, within seconds. Some sites have statistics that are delayed by 20 minutes or an hour. That is acceptable. You can live with that. Real-time sales reporting is another good reason to do business with merchants in affiliate networks like Commission Junction. To be competitive, most of the affiliate networks provide real-time reporting to their merchants and affiliates. Being part of the network means that you do not have to hunt around to find out whether real-time reporting is a feature of the program that you want to join.

Does the Merchant Offer Sales Copy and Other Tools? Most merchants offer their affiliates advertising copy and banner ads for placement on their sites. In many cases, you will be able to generate the code with a click of your mouse, which you then paste into your page or in your newsletter. Some merchants also offer product data feeds for their entire range of products. Using data feeds, you can build a 1,000-item site in mere seconds!

Many merchants also host the banners from their own sites, which saves you the trouble of downloading and saving the graphic to your computer and then uploading it to your server. Banners that are kept on the merchant's server also reduce your bandwidth. The downside is that the merchant can change the banner or remove it altogether without your knowledge. Sales tools make an affiliate's job easier.

How and When Do I Get Paid? Payments are usually by check or direct deposit, although some companies pay in merchandise or service credits.

PayPal.com This vehicle has become a very popular payment method for many merchants. Paypal is an account-based system that lets anyone with an e-mail address send and receive online payments securely using credit cards or bank accounts.

When given the option of taking a check or payment from PayPal, it is better to take the check because PayPal's fees eat into your commissions. Some merchants will not give you the option, however, so it is best to sign up for a PayPal account at PayPal. com.

Most Internet companies do business and pay in U.S. dollars. Be sure to confirm the currency in which the company deals. Ken Evoy's 5 Pillar Affiliate program is based in Canada. Affiliates are automatically paid in Canadian dollars if they live in Canada and American dollars if they live anywhere else in the world. His program allows affiliates to change that option if they are Canadians who prefer to be paid in U.S. dollars.

Payment Schedules Programs can pay weekly, biweekly, monthly, and quarterly. Many programs require that you earn a minimum amount before they will issue you a check. For example, some merchants set their minimum payouts at $50 or $100. This makes sense if your earnings for the month are $2 and it costs the merchant $5 to cut you a check. Other merchants give you a choice of minimum commission amounts, which is advantageous to overseas affiliates who have to pay bank fees on U.S. dollar checks. Compensation plans vary from merchant to merchant and program to program. Be sure you know what the payment plan is, or you could be in for a nasty surprise.

Does the Merchant Use Third-Party Billing? One nice thing about associating with merchants who are part of a bigger affiliate network is that you can count on the affiliate network to make sure that the merchants have put enough money into their account to pay your commissions. Some networks go so far as to indicate how well each merchant's account is funded, allowing you to choose whether or not you should promote their products. Other networks will suspend the merchants' account until they have deposited sufficient funds. You do not get that kind of security when you sign up for a program that is administered by the company itself. While you do not need to worry about Amazon or Match .com, it is sometimes hard to be sure about smaller companies that you do not know.

One way to gain security is to ask whether the company uses third-party billing to process its payments and handle affiliate commissions. A third-party processor takes in money from the customers and makes sure that the affiliates receive what is due to them. Beware. Depending on the affiliate agreement, you may end up splitting the payment processing costs with the merchant, which can lower your commission split by up to 50 percent.

Are Co-branded Sites Available to Affiliates? Co-branding is a form of customization in which the affiliate program permits you to "brand" a copy of the landing page on its site with your logo and/or your site's "look and feel." Visiting a co-branded site gives your visitors the impression they are still on your Web site and may improve visitor trust in your products, resulting in increased sales.

Many merchants offered co-branding when affiliate marketing first began on the Net. However, few merchants offer co-branding nowadays. It is simply too much work for them to approve each and every affiliate's logo graphic. For sites that allowed affiliates to automatically upload logos, there was always the potential that the logo was inappropriate and/or not in keeping with the image the company wanted to maintain.

To Join or Not to Join? If the answer to your question is not on the merchant's site, phone or e-mail to get what you need. If contact information is not prominently displayed on the Web site, find another program to join. Also, if you do not get a response within a reasonable time frame, say 24 to 48 hours, then find another program to join. On the other hand, make sure that the answer to your question is not included in the affiliate package before contacting the program manager. Such managers are busy people, and you won't want to make a poor first impression by wasting their time with unnecessary questions. Ask all the right questions and make sure the affiliate programs are solid prospects before you join.

MERCHANT HAS NO AFFILIATE PROGRAM

If you find great products that do not appear to be supported by an affiliate program, it is time to put your knowledge of affiliate marketing to work. Phone or e-mail the merchants, tell them how much you love their product, and ask if they have an affiliate program. (See Figure 9.3.) If they say that they do not, or do not know what affiliate programs are, you will have to explain the concept and process to them.

Figure 9.3 Sample E-Mail

Dear (merchant's name),

I just visited (merchant's URL) and think that (company name)'s (specific products) are absolutely fabulous!
I would love the opportunity to sell them on my (site theme) at (site URL). However, I wasn't able to find affiliate program information at (merchant's URL),

Does (company name) have an affiliate program? If so, would you be so kind as to send me the sign-up URL?

If there is no affiliate program, would you be interested in an affiliate partnership with (site URL)? Our site receives (number) visitors a day who are interested in (site theme) goods. I know they'd also love (company name)'s products.

If you are interested, please feel free to contact me if you have any questions about how to start an affiliate program for (site URL). I have personal experience with affiliate programs and can help save you time and money in getting set up.

Thanks for your consideration, and I look forward to hearing from you.

Sincerely,

(your name)

(your name)
(your company name)
(your URL)
(address and telephone number)

Figure 9.4   Sample E-Mail

Dear (merchant's name),

I am very pleased that you are interested in an affiliate alliance with (your URL) to promote (company name)'s products. I know you will be thrilled with how affiliate marketing will increase your sales.

There are three different ways to set up an affiliate program.

Join an affiliate network that handles almost all the work associated with the program, including processing orders and affiliate payments. This is perhaps the most costly solution, but it requires the least effort and will put (company name)'s products in front of thousands of affiliates eager to sell your product.

Sign up with a shopping cart service that includes affiliate-tracking software. Although less expensive, this option is slightly more work in that you will need to advertise the program to gain more affiliates.

Buy and install affiliate program software on your own server. This option is the least expensive with a one-time purchase of software, but the most time-consuming to administer in terms of keeping track of affiliate sales and payment handling.

To learn more, here is a page that lists a variety of affiliate management solutions. I also recommend Ralph Wilson's "Report on Affiliate Management Software," which spells out different options in great detail.

(Continued)

Figure 9.4 (Continued)

If after reviewing those sites you have questions, please feel free to contact me.

I look forward to working with you.

Sincerely,

(your name)

(your name)
(your company name)
(your URL)
(address and telephone number)

If the company responds saying that it is interested in a partnership, you might consider sending another e-mail similar to the one in Figure 9.4.

Figures 9.3 and 9.4 are sample e-mails. Feel free to adjust the wording to your needs. Enter your own affiliate ID codes into the links for the sites you recommend.

AFFILIATING WITH BOOKSTORES

Adding books to your site that are relevant to your topic is a smart thing to do. Most folks are online looking for information or entertainment, and what is more informative and entertaining than a book? It is a good plan, but there are drawbacks.

Selling books online is not usually a profitable venture. Amazon's top commission rate is 15 percent of the sale. That amount is reduced to 5 percent if the visitor arrives at Amazon from a specific product link on your site but then buys a different product. Most bookstores' top commission rate is only 5 percent. Five percent of $10 is 50 cents. If you sell thousands of books, you can earn a nice chunk of change. However, if the books on your site qualify as an "additional" offering through Amazon, it is unlikely that you will ever make a significant sum of money by selling books through their affiliate program. Although it is true that every little bit counts, if your main product pays you a commission of $20 per sale and your book links draw attention away from the main focus of your site, having an onsite library may diminish your total income.

GOOGLE ADSENSE: AN ALTERNATIVE TO PRODUCT SALES

Google's AdSense is a quick and easy way to generate revenue from a content-rich Web site. It all starts with Google Adwords, in which advertisers pay Google to have their ads appear next to search results. For example, if you type the search term "cosmetics" into the Google search engine, in addition to the regular listings in the main body of the page, a number of ads for cosmetics appear in the sponsored links section on the right side of the search results page.

Google's AdSense program provides those advertisers with additional reach by putting their ads onto the search results pages and Web sites with complementary content. That is where you, as an affiliate, can benefit. Google will pay you a commission for running the ads on your site. Anytime someone clicks on one of those ads on your Web pages, you will earn a piece of the Google pie. Google's Web spiders, or the programs that evaluate your site's content, relate the ads they display to the content of your Web page. Therein lies the art behind making Adsense work for you.

The object is to write page content focused on a specific theme, targeting one or two keywords or keyword phrases. Adsense then rewards you with ads related to the content of that page. Because your visitors are already interested in that topic, they are more likely to click on the ad, and bingo! You earn a commission for the click.

How much commission? Google does not publish those amounts. Its reasons may have something to do with the legal contracts between Google and its premium distribution partners. Estimates put the rates between 40 and 60 percent of Adwords rates and Adsense earnings.

Although Google's Adsense terms of agreement prohibit Adsense publishers from reporting their earnings, tales of riches abound. Recently Google AdSense has relaxed that rule so more webmasterss are publishing their monthly AdSense revenue (usually as a way to entice you to buy their book about how to improve AdSense revenue).

- Chris Pirillo, best-selling author and creator of the Lockergnome series of online publications, reports clearing more than $10,000 a month.

- Jason Calacanis says that his sites made $45,000 within the first four months of launch.

- With permission from Google, Joel Comm displays a screenshot of his AdSense stats page for November 2004 on his "AdSense Secrets" (http://Adsense-Secrets.com) site showing earnings of $25,983.02 for the month. To enjoy a piece of that pie, visit Google Adsense (https://www.google.com/adsense) to set up an account. You will be given a piece of code to include in every page of your Web site where you want AdSense ads to appear. Once visitors start clicking those ads, you will be earning Adsense revenue.

10

Market Your Site

In the early days of Internet marketing, attracting visitors to a new site was free, fast, and easy. Sites that were submitted to Yahoo!, AltaVista, Excite, and other search engines would see their homepages listed on the first page of results within a matter of days. Traffic started flowing in, and so did the sales. Unfortunately, the days of fast and easy search engine listing are gone. You can now wait months for your site to get spidered by the free search engines, and end up on the 40th or 340th page of search engine returns for your most important keyword phrases.

Even if your site shows up in the 50th spot, on the second page of results, you will not earn enough from the paltry traffic to buy lunch, let alone groceries. It is surprising therefore how many newbie Internet marketers still wait patiently for what can be months for their site to get listed by the free search engines rather than use multiple marketing methods to bring traffic to their sites.

In the following section, you will learn about a number of ways to bring those all-important visitors to your site—some of which start delivering traffic in minutes.

PAY-PER-CLICK ADVERTISING

Pay-per-click advertising should top your list of marketing strategies. Pay-per-click (or cost-per-click) advertising enables you to place an ad for your Web site, product, or service on the Net related to keywords or keyword phrases you select. You bid for positioning of your ad on the search engine results pages. Each time a customer clicks on your ad, you pay the price you have bid, regardless of whether the customer buys your product or service.

The two big players in the pay-per-click industry are Google AdWords and Yahoo! Search Marketing (formerly Overture). There are also hundreds of other smaller pay-per-click search engines. How does pay-per-click advertising work? The amount you bid for pay-per-click advertising is based on the popularity of the keyword or key phrase you are bidding on; that is, how many people bid on your ad and the quality of the ad. The more you are willing to spend per click, the higher your site will appear in the results for the keywords you choose.

With Google AdWords and Yahoo! Search Marketing your ad must also be popular and of high quality; otherwise your ranking can fall. The fastest way to get exposure online is by advertising with Google Adwords. Ads start running within minutes after you submit your billing information.

Google is the number one search engine used by surfers, and more importantly, online shoppers. Google Adwords are the "Sponsored Listings" that you see displayed in small rectangle boxes running down the right side of the Google search results page. Google Adwords has already attracted hundreds of thousands of advertisers, and for good reason. It is a quick and simple way to purchase highly targeted cost-per-click (CPC) advertising. Your ads may be shown on search results pages for Google, Google Directory, Google Groups, and Google's partner sites, including the partners' directory results pages. You may choose to have your ads shown only for search results on Google, if you do not want to participate in the syndication program. Google's advertising network includes sites like AOL, CompuServe, Netscape, Ask.com, AT&T Worldnet, EarthLink, and Excite.

To create a Google AdWords ad, write a description, choose keywords that are relevant to the listing, and specify the maximum amount you are willing to pay for each click. Google AdWords has a tool to help you with relevant keywords relating to the word or phrase you have chosen.

To save money, the AdWords Discounter automatically reduces the actual cost per click you pay to the lowest cost needed to maintain your ad's position on the results page. There is no minimum monthly charge for Google Adwords, just a $5 activation fee. You can easily keep track of your ad performance using the reports in your online account Control Center.

AdWords Select's best feature is that it rewards advertisers who draw clicks by giving them better positioning. Your ad's position on the page depends in part on how often the ad is clicked on by users. So, the better the ad, the higher up on the page it appears. Conversely, if your ad is not drawing clicks, AdWords Select (https://adwords.google

.com/select/) will penalize you by lowering your ranking on the search page and increasing your bid price. The Google Adwords campaign system is highly flexible. At the campaign level, you choose your daily budget, geotargeting, syndication preference, and start and end dates.

After signing up for your Google Adwords account, sign up for accounts at the following:

- Yahoo! Search Marketing: http://searchmarketing.yahoo.com
- MIVA Marketplace: http://mivamarketplace.com
- Enhance Interactive: http://www.enhance.com/pay-per-click-advertising.html

These are the top three pay-per-click search engines in terms of traffic volume. Yahoo! Search Marketing's minimum bid is 19 cents and, like Google, there is no monthly minimum spend amount. Allan Gardyne's PayPerClickSearchEngines.com site lists 537 PPC search engines with relevant information on each of them. The very popular PPC search engines often are a lot more expensive than their smaller, cheaper counterparts.

E-MAIL MARKETING

Permission-based e-mail marketing works! Because your subscribers have voluntarily signed up or "opted in" to receive your information, they are interested in what you have to say. Sending regular e-mails to your opt-in list allows you to:

- Offer products and services for sale to your subscribers.
- Survey subscribers to gather information for new products.
- Build a rapport with your subscribers.

Studies have shown that permission e-mail yields response rates that are 10 times better than banners.

Use Autoresponders

Once you have built a list of a few hundred subscribers, keeping that list up-to-date on an ongoing basis can be a complicated and time-consuming process. Use a professional mailing list or autoresponder service to keep track of your subscribers and broadcast your messages. These services automatically handle all your sign-ups, unsubscriptions, and bounced e-mails.

The biggest advantage to having a professional service maintain your mailing list is that it protects you from spam complaints. Most affiliate networks that permit e-mail marketing of their merchants' offerings insist that you be able to produce evidence of subscriber opt-in. Most professional mailing list services also provide a "double opt-in service." This means that after your customers sign up for your newsletter on your Web site, they are automatically sent an acknowledgement letter requesting that they confirm their desire to be on your mailing list. This is a surefire way to guarantee that your subscriber genuinely wants to receive your e-mails.

Under the CAN-SPAM Act, which became effective on January 1, 2004, companies are liable for illegal spam sent by their affiliates. As such, most affiliate networks that permit e-mail marketing of their merchants' offerings insist that you be able to produce evidence of subscriber opt-in. Spam wastes everyone's time and energy. The "do unto others" rule is a good one to follow when contemplating the use of unsolicited e-mail.

Using a mailing list service will also prevent having your Internet service provider (ISP) close your account down because you sucked up too much of its bandwidth by sending 30,000 e-mails to your subscribers. To set up your opt-in mailing list, Aweber.com offers one of the best autoresponder services on the Net.

Publish an E-Course and a Newsletter

Many Internet marketers use a free e-course as incentive to get visitors to join their mailing list. An e-course is a series of autoresponder messages or set of preprogrammed messages that are sent to subscribers at specified intervals. The first message is delivered immediately upon sign up.

In addition to the e-course, your subscribers will also receive your broadcast messages or newsletter. Published regularly, a good newsletter brings visitors back to your site over and over again, exposing them to all the wonderful products and services you have to offer. Use your newsletter to notify your subscribers about special promotions and sales held by your merchant partners. It is best to link from your newsletter to a special sales page on your site, as opposed to sending customers directly to the merchant's site. That way you can test the effectiveness of your offers by keeping track of the number of visitors who visit that page via your newsletter.

Once you have built a substantial subscriber list, the effect is fairly immediate and is always positive. People rush off to the site to take advantage of the offer, and you get a nice little bonus for doing a small amount of work. If you think that building a subscriber list and sending newsletters is too much work, consider the following example carefully.

Suppose that 5,000 visitors arrive at your Web site in an average week. Even though they have an interest in your site's subject, the vast majority of these people will never return to your site because they will forget about it or will not remember how to get there. Imagine if you had a free newsletter or course to offer them in exchange for their name and e-mail address. At a sign-up rate of

---

SUPER AFFILIATE TIP

"Cloaking links" are often used in e-mails because the affiliate links given by 1ShoppingCart and MyAffiliateProgram are so long that they may be broken by the time they get to the recipient. Your link for 1ShoppingCart affiliate link may look like this:

[http://www.1shoppingcart.com/app/default.asp?pr=1&id=63306]

Some e-mail programs will wrap the line, and the link ends up looking like this:

[http://www.1shoppingcart.com/app/default.
asp?pr=1&id=63306]

Recipients click on the first part of the link and get a "Page Cannot be Found" error, which diminishes their trust in you immediately. You will also lose the sale.

You may therefore want to invest in link cloaking software such as Affiliate Link Cloaker (http://www.affiliatelink-cloaker.com) to shorten those long affiliate links.

The other option is to use the TinyUrl.com (http://www.tinyurl.com) service. Using TinyUrl.com, the 1ShoppingCart link above turned into:

[http://tinyurl.com/s6nd4]

10 percent, you would be getting 500 new opt-in subscribers per week, or 6,000 per year!

GIVE YOUR ARTICLES AWAY

E-zine and Web site advertising can be expensive, each ad costing anywhere from a few dollars to thousands of dollars. However, marketing your articles by submitting them to e-zine publishers and article directories costs nothing more than your time, and this will attract visitors to your site in droves. When your articles are published in relevant e-zines and on article directories, people who are interested in your subject matter will read them. Interested readers become visitors, who in turn become motivated purchasers, and then repeat buyers. Depending on the subscriber base of the e-zine that uses your article, or traffic to the article directory, the potential for bringing new visitors to your site can be enormous.

Simply write a short how-to article on a topic relevant to your Web site topic. At the end of each article, add your byline, or "author's resource box," with your personal bio and your site's URL. To get your article published in e-zines, look for sites with topics that are complementary to your own, not direct competitors. Best E-zines (http://bestezines.com) has a listing of 1,155 of the best e-zines, servicing over 1,250,000 subscribers. Search the categories for those related to your topic and send the webmaster one of your favorite articles with your bio and a link back to your site.

Onsite archiving of e-zines has an additional benefit. Your site's popularity increases as links to your site appear on more and more pages. With increased exposure, your name becomes better known, and your credibility as an expert grows. This effect becomes cumulative, because experts are frequently interviewed for other publications, which again increases their popularity.

Article Directories

Placing your articles on article directories is even easier to do because you do not need to contact the site's webmaster directly to solicit interest in your material. Article directories generally have submission pages on which you simply fill out a form that includes fields for your name, e-mail address, URL, title of the article, the article body, and your byline.

Different directories have different formatting requirements. Some require straight text insertions, while others want the article in HTML format. A few directory webmasters will ask you to provide an autoresponder address through which their visitors can have the article sent to them via e-mail. Although some article submission sites will ask for your specific terms of use or author's guidelines, articles placed on most directories are freely available to other webmasters s for use on their sites according to the rules of that particular directory. Figure 10.1 provides a short list of article submission sites to get you started.

Figure 10.1 Article Submission Sites

Article Announce	http://groups.yahoo.com/group/article_announce
Free Content	http://groups.yahoo.com/group/free-content
Idea Marketers	http://www.ideamarketers.com
Marketing Seek	http://www.marketing-seek.com

Last but not least, offer your articles as free content to other webmasters. Make sure to add your author's guidelines and stipulate whether you want to be contacted for permission to use your articles.

Article Submission Software

Submitting your articles to individual directories can be somewhat time-consuming and tedious. To speed up the process considerably and gain even more exposure, a worthwhile program is Jason Potash's "Article Announcer" software. Article Announcer is Jason Potash's training course manuals with added software to help you with every facet of how to create, outsource, optimize, and promote your articles for maximum results, all while streamlining the whole process for you.

The software makes it easy to:

- Submit your articles to article directories.
- Submit your articles to article announcements lists.
- Perform automatic word count.
- Format.
- Spam check to help your articles get through spam filters.
- Keep track of your submissions.

It also includes an invaluable "Article Blueprint" audio, which is a four-hour session with Jason Potash and John Reese on the essentials of article writing, traffic generation, and the art of article distribution. In addition to a huge selection of editors, directories, and lists to which you can submit your work, you can add your own resources to the Article Announcer software as you find them.

GET LISTED IN THE SEARCH ENGINES

There is an approach to affiliate marketing that focuses almost exclusively on search engine marketing as its primary method of driving traffic. The approach involves building tens and hundreds of little sites around topics that are chosen not out of interest, but for pure profit potential. Each site may make a paltry $20 to $100 per month. The content on these sites is typically written according to a keyword density formula that involves repetitive use of chosen keywords and keyword phrases throughout the article.

Besides the fact that this method of writing usually results in dull, uninformative drivel that adds useless Web clutter and does little or nothing to actually inform the site's visitors, this method has repeatedly proven to be unsustainable. Many affiliates who use this technique have had their sites deranked and/or delisted by search engines such as Google, which do their best to keep such formulaic Web sites out of search engine results.

Because these affiliates relied primarily on search engine traffic, their $40,000 per month incomes plummeted to less than $1,000 per month overnight, when their traffic dried up completely. Many have since given up on affiliate marketing and returned to day jobs. Do your best to bring free traffic to your sites, but hedge your bets and combine those efforts with paid advertising, and implement the suggestions in the "Make Your Pages Search Engine Friendly" section of Chapter 8.

Add a Blog to Your Web Site

Regular blogging is one of the best methods for attracting free search engine traffic and keeping your visitors interested in your site. Blog entries are typically shorter than newsletters or articles and can be used to quickly post new merchant offers or deliver the latest industry news. Search engines seem to love blog entries. It is quite common to hear of webmasters who have added blog entries on one day and have had them listed in the top search entries for the particular search phrase they've focused on by the next day.

Blogging tends to be less formal than articles or newsletters. You can be more personal, outrageous, controversial, or just plain funny in your blogs. Do not be afraid to add some of your character to your blog posts. It is a great way of capturing your visitor's attention and attracting more visitors to and interest in your site. Newsworthy blogs create publicity, and news has a habit of traveling fast on the Internet! Using Aweber's (http://www.aweber.com) RSS to e-mail technology, you can also have blog posts delivered automatically to your newsletter subscribers, giving them still more reason to revisit your site.

Most blogging software is free and simple to install and upload to your server. I recommend WordPress (http://www.wordpress.com) as the most user-friendly and efficient of the blogging tools available.

Only after you start getting copious amounts of traffic to your site and are making copious amounts of money should you even think about spending time tweaking your meta tags for better search engine placement. In order to do this, your pages must be properly optimized. Page optimization and submissions are dealt with in more detail in "Include Meta Tags" in the "Make Your Pages Search Engine Friendly" section in Chapter 8.

Search engine crawlers visit sites and automatically build listings, generally without the need to submit your site. Crawler-based search engines use automated software agents (called crawlers) that visit a Web site, read the site's meta tags, and also follow the links that the site connects to. The crawler returns that information back to the engine where the data is indexed. The crawler returns to the site periodically to check for changes. One of the quickest ways to get a visit from Google's spider is to have a paid listing in the Yahoo! directory. Submit your pages to the search engines regularly. (The jury is still out on whether you need to submit your pages to the search engines every few months or whether once is enough.)

If you suddenly notice that a page that was ranking well in the search engines has suddenly disappeared or has lost rankings, it may need to be resubmitted. However, as long as you are regularly updating your content, the search engine spiders will be visiting regularly looking for fresh food to add to their search results.

Following is a list of search engines where you may want to submit your sites and pages.

- Google.com (http://www.google.com/addurl.html)
- MSN.com (http://search. msn.com/docs/submit.aspx?FORM= WSDD2)
- AskJeeves.com (http://www.askjeeves.com)
- AlltheWeb (http://www.alltheweb.com/add_url.php)
- AltaVista (http://addurl.altavista.com/addurl/default)
- DMOZ (http://www.dmoz.org/add.html)

DMOZ is not a search engine. It is a human-edited Web directory similar to a huge reference library. It is highly selective about the listings it accepts and there are real advantages to being listed in DMOZ. Although it is a free service, there are no guarantees that your site will be listed. You may have to wait a long time before being accepted.

The advantages come from the fact that the search engines favor sites that have been listed in the DMOZ directory and you can earn valuable brownie points simply by being listed there. It is certainly worth submitting your URL details, but do not hold your breath while you wait to see if your site gets listed any time within the first three to six months. To learn more about how the search engines work, visit SearchEngineWatch.com.

Using Submission Services and Software

A keyword search for "Web site submission" or "submission services" at Google or Yahoo! yields hundreds of companies offering to submit your site to the search engines for a fee. Many of these services promise to hand-submit your site to hundreds of engines all for the unbelievably low price of $9—or for incredibly good value at $999. You should know that there are only a handful of important search engines and that you can submit to these yourself for free. There is also software that will submit your sites to the search engines. However, here is a warning from Google about using such software.

> Do not use unauthorized computer programs to submit pages, check rankings, etc. Such programs consume computing resources and violate our terms of service. Google does not recommend the use of products such as WebPosition Gold™ that send automatic or programmatic queries to Google.

The point to remember here is not to waste your hard-earned money on search engine submission services or programs. The only search engines that matter in terms of a site's search engine results are those mentioned, and all welcome free submissions.

BUY A DIRECTORY LISTING AT YAHOO!

At the time of this writing, Yahoo! charges $299 (nonrefundable) for its Yahoo! Express expedited listing service, and $600 for adult-oriented sites. Most webmasters consider that a small price to pay for the large volume of traffic that Yahoo! can send to their site.

Payment does not guarantee inclusion in the directory. It only guarantees that a member of Yahoo!'s editorial staff will look at your site, consider your suggestion to include the site in the directory, and respond to you within seven business days from the date that you submit your site for consideration letting you know whether your site will be added or denied. If your listing is denied, you have the right to appeal and/or make changes to your site within a certain amount of time and resubmit without making an additional payment. If your site is accepted, you will be charged $299 the following year and each subsequent year to maintain the listing.

It is well worth the money to list your site with Yahoo! Being listed in Yahoo's handpicked, human-compiled directory is one of the best ways to make sure that Google crawls and picks up your home-page quickly. A link from Yahoo! will also improve your Google page rank. Even without the Yahoo! link, Google will find your page eventually, but if you are looking for lots of traffic fast, a Yahoo! listing will get you there.

ISSUE PRESS RELEASES

Whenever you have an event scheduled or breaking news related to your site's topic, send out a press release and announce it to the world. For example, as a dog training site webmaster you might discover that 70 percent of visitors to your site have won their local dog show events or that the rate of new dog training clubs has suddenly increased. Report such information in a press release.

A well-written release can dramatically increase your sales, expose your company to the masses, and greatly enhance the image of your business or products. Press release and news services like PRWeb.com offer a comprehensive guide to writing an effective and newsworthy press release that will get you and your site noticed.

PARTICIPATE IN GROUPS AND FORUMS

Forums are like message boards where members post messages for the entire group to read. Most forums are focused around a central theme. Yahoo!, Google, MSN, and other major portal sites have discussion groups and clubs to which you can post messages. Many new webmasters lurk in forums, afraid to post either questions or comment.

Do not be afraid to post. No one will bite provided you follow the rules. Even if you accidentally break one of the rules, chances are that you will be politely reminded of the rules, asked to follow them in the future, and given another chance to participate. Responding to another group member's question with valuable information is the best way to gain respect and credibility in the groups.

To profit from forums, find and participate in ones related to your industry. Place your site's URL in your signature line. When you provide stellar information, people will want to hear more of what you have to say and will click on that link.

Following are general guidelines for posting on forums.

- *Place your comments in the correct category.* Many forums have a variety of different topic sections. Be sure to post your messages and questions in the right section.

- *Refrain from posting.* Refrain from posting questions or duplicating answers that have already been answered numerous times; negative or aggressive remarks (i.e., flames) directed toward other users; anything not relating to the original topic; any derogatory comments based on age, gender, race, ethnicity, or nationality.

- *Post only useful information.* A post that says, "Anyone in here?" wastes time when the number of viewers who read the post is taken into consideration. Make intelligent posts that have a purpose.

- *Obey copyright rules.* Respect the law and do not post copyrighted work unless you have written permission from its owner.

- *Do not promote your own site, unless this is permitted by the forum rules.* Many webmasters permit promotional items in a specific area of their forum.

- *Do not spam the forum.* Spam includes advertisements, content deemed inappropriate or illegal, and flooding of the boards (repeated and/or multiple "unnecessary" postings).

- *Use a signature file.* Create a signature file (a short block of text at the end of a message that identifies the sender and provides additional information about him or her) that is a reasonable size and does not contain excessively large images or annoying animations, and follows all the rules applying to the posts themselves. Check to see what frequent posters to the forum have included in their signature files.

- *Respect the privacy of others.* Do not post private addresses or phone numbers, including your own.

- Avoid needless use of

Emoticons

Line breaks or ALL-CAPS

Nested quotes

Giant fonts

Swearing, derogatory terms, hate-speech, obscene or vulgar comments (Probably the most effective way to receive a permanent or temporary ban.)

Finally, if you have problems, just make a post in the appropriate forum, and somebody will almost certainly be glad to help you.

Some of the most useful and busy affiliate marketing forums are listed here.

- *ABestWeb.*   Variety of entrepreneurial topics in a continuous thread presentation from the homepage. Search options available and preferences can be set. (http://www.abestweb.com/)
- *Associate Programs Forum.*   Allan Gardyne's forum is a great source of information about affiliate programs from those who use them. Allan frequently shares sound advice in his own inimitable, levelheaded style. (http://associateprograms.com/discus)
- *How to Forum.*   Michael Green's forum is touted as the world's largest Internet marketing forum where Internet marketers can exchange ideas, ask questions, and get the answers they are looking for. (http://www.howtocorp.com/forum)
- *NetProfitsToday Forum.* Rosalind Gardner's NPT "Forumites" are generous with their time and helpful advice! (http://www.netprofitstoday.com /forum)

> ## SUPER AFFILIATE TIP
>
> Learn about affiliate and Internet marketing from others and share your own knowledge. Visit a forum, ask questions, and speak up!

PLACE ADS IN RELEVANT NEWSLETTERS AND E-ZINES

Tens if not hundreds of thousands of e-zines and newsletters are published on the Internet. Advertising in e-zines that are relevant to your site's topic is a low cost and extremely effective way to attract interested visitors to your site. The Directory of E-zines is an excellent resource for quickly finding e-zines targeted to your audience. For a wealth of information about e-mail advertising and to access targeted opt-in e-mail lists where you can place your ads, visit BestEzines.com, DirectoryofEzines.com, and e-zinez.com.

PROMOTE AFFILIATE SITES ON eBAY

As an affiliate, you cannot sell your products directly on eBay because you do not own the products you promote; you merely send qualified leads to your merchant's site. But there is a simple three-step process you can use to tap into the huge eBay marketplace.

Step 1

Find e-books, products, or software with reprint or reseller rights, preferably related to your site's content, which you can repackage and sell as you wish. You can even create your own e-book or report that you can sell cheaply. Be sure that the product contains plenty of *your* affiliate links that will take customers to *your* affiliate merchants.

Make the book or product fully and easily downloadable by using a PDF format and offering to e-mail the downloadable item to your purchaser. Write a compelling title and text for your product. Research what terms people are looking for and what other affiliates are saying about their products, and then use their expertise (or lack of it!) to write your own story.

Step 2

Following eBay's instructions, upload your item to the eBay auction site, using the "Buy It Now!" option. You don't want to simply sell one of your products; you want to sell as many as possible, so select the multiple items fixed-price option. (Make sure you choose to include the "counter" so that you will be able to see how many browsers you are getting compared with buyers.)

The profit margin is not your true goal. Getting your buyers to click on the affiliate links to your product is part of the grand plan, so make the price reasonable—even cheap—so that your visitors believe they are getting an absolute bargain. Use PayPal as your banker.

eBay forbids you from linking directly to your site from an eBay auction page, so build an "About Me" page by clicking on the eBay community link. In the same way that you wrote a friendly, conversational, and refreshingly open page on your Web site titled "About Us," write something similar for eBay. In that way you can include a link back to your site.

Step 3

You are not going to make a fortune by selling rebrandable e-books at $4.99 each. Nor is it likely that your buyers will click on all the affiliate links you've placed within the e-book. What you should do is dangle a carrot on your eBay About Us page about a free product that you have available on your Web site. You've already managed to get the e-mail addresses of your buyers; what you want now is the e-mail addresses of the browsers. Your visitors and customers can receive the report in exchange for an e-mail address. The product could be a simple five-page report or another product for which you have the resale rights.

Using your autoresponder, set up a series of e-mails promoting your product(s) and services. The first e-mail in the series could simply be a thank-you message offering a freebie just for looking at your site. This is a trial-and-error process that takes a little time to set up, and you will have to tweak your auction page, title, about us page, and maybe even your autoresponder messages.

However, once you find a system and e-mail sequence that works, you can use it as your major tool to tap into the vast resources eBay has made available to you. Register to become a seller at any or all of the online auction sites listed below:

- http://eBay.com.au (Australia)
- http://eBay.ca (Canada)
- http://ebay.co.uk (United Kingdom)
- http://eBay.com (United States)
- http://uBid.com
- http://auctions.shopping.yahoo.com

GET FREE DIRECTORY LISTINGS

Getting a listing in a general directory or one specifically related to your topic can prove to be very beneficial. Many of the directories have high Google Page Rank, which means that a one-way listing in these directories carries a lot of weight with Google. Unfortunately, most of the best directories charge a fee (anywhere from $10 to $150), but you will find that your outlay is recouped quickly with increased search traffic and a better Google Page Rank.

Smaller search directories still trying to build their database may offer a free service, but they will request a reciprocal link in return. The Yahoo! (http://search.yahoo.com/info/submit.html) directory does not accept free listings in its commercial categories, so affiliate sites, which are commercial sites, are not be eligible for free listings.

Some affiliate marketing coaches will suggest that you should apply for a Yahoo! directory listing once you have content on your site but before your affiliate links are in place. That is nothing more than a scam tactic and a dangerous one at that. The Yahoo! directory is constantly being reviewed for relevancy. What would happen if you use this tactic, start earning decent commissions, and then suddenly have your listing removed when the reviewer discovers that it is in fact an affiliate site? First, your earnings will decrease. And second, you will not be able to count on having the site approved for a commercial listing after you tried to scam Yahoo!

REALLY SIMPLE SYNDICATION (RSS)

Really Simple Syndication, or Rich Site Summary is a way for you to publish dynamic, self-updating content with very little effort. These feeds are also referred to as Headline Syndication, Aggregators, and XML Format. Many Web sites now use RSS feeds to publish updates about themselves. A single news item will typically include a headline, which instantly informs the reader of what the page contains, and a snippet of content (usually the first few lines of the article), with a link to your site.

From the Net entrepreneur's point of view, an RSS feed provides visitors and subscribers with an easy way to keep themselves abreast of fresh content on your Web site (without having them visit the Web site first). Additionally, an RSS feed also allows readers to preview this fresh content, thus letting them decide immediately if the new article or content is interesting to them or not. All in all, the main purpose of RSS feeds is to enhance the user experience.

One of your most valuable tools can be an RSS reader. This is essentially an aggregator—a collection of RSS feeds (that you can add or remove) from different Web sites that you are interested in. A typical RSS reader would include RSS feeds from news sites, sports sites, and perhaps a few niche sites that are related to your Web site topics. The main purpose of this software is to keep you and your visitors informed of the latest news and content on Web sites that you are interested in.

RSS is an amazingly versatile tool that can be used for something as simple as running a latest news page on your site to something as time-sensitive as running a stock price ticker. There are many RSS feed readers, also known as "aggregators," to choose from. Two of the best are My Yahoo! (http://my.yahoo.com) and Bloglines (http://www.bloglines.com). By simply doing a search for "RSS readers," you will find many other aggregators to choose from.

SOCIAL BOOKMARKING

Web sites like technorati.com and del.icio.us that provide "social bookmarking" pages are the latest craze on the Net. Social bookmarking is a simple way of displaying your favorite sites online, rather than in the Favorites tab in your Web browser. You set up on your own special page where you can usually include your personal profile, then bookmark all your favorite sites in one place (including your own!). This information is available across the Web to anyone searching for your specific tags or bookmarks.

The major advantage of adding your own Web pages or blogs to a social bookmarking page is that the social bookmarking site will reward you by giving you a powerful link back to your own Web site. Another example of the power of social bookmarking is if a group of like-minded people bookmark all their favorite dog training sites, including yours, you have a wide-ranging list of links back to your site, bringing with them more targeted traffic.

Social bookmarking, tagging, and pinging are relatively new. The best way to learn about how the social bookmarking phenomenon can help you increase rankings and attract more free traffic is to read Sean Wu's informational e-book *The Tag and Ping Blueprint* at http://www.tagandping.com.

USE AN E-MAIL SIGNATURE

An e-mail signature line advertises your site each time you send an e-mail. Your e-mail signature can be formatted as is shown in Figure 10.2.

Create a Signature File

You can develop a signature file in Microsoft Outlook by following these directions:

- Open Outlook.
- Under the tools menu, click on "options."

Figure 10.2 Sample format for E-Mail Signature

Full name
Company name
Street address
City, state/province, zip/postal code
Phone:
Fax:
E-mail address
Site URL address

- Click the "mail format" tab.
- Click "signature picker" at the bottom of the screen.
- Choose "new" and follow the prompts to name your signature file.

Once you make the new signature file the default, it will be inserted automatically at the end of every e-mail you send, thus generating referral fees without any further work on your part.

Create a Signature File in Eudora

Another option is to use Eudora to create your signature file. Follow these directions:

- Open Eudora.
- Under tools, click on "signatures." This will open the signatures box on the left side of your screen.
- Right-click in the box, and select "new."

- A box pops open titled "Create New Signature" and prompts you to "enter signature name" in the form. Choose a name for your new signature, and then click OK.

- A blank page opens. Type your promotional message and URL in this space. You have the option to be creative with font colors, sizes, and types. When you're finished, click file, and then save.

To set your new signature as the default signature, choose "options" under the tools menu, then "composing mail." In the drop down box beside "signature," pick the name you chose for your new signature.

MARKET YOUR SITE OFFLINE

Marketing your affiliate Web sites offline can be a hit-and-miss affair. In most cases it's a waste of time and money, and time is money. However, there are many affiliate webmasters who will attest to the power of word of mouth.

Print Business Cards

Business cards are highly effective marketing tools when you remember to put them in your wallet. Use every opportunity to pass on one of your business cards to everyone and anyone who seems interested.

Be sure that your business card includes your URL, name, and e-mail address so that people can get in touch with you easily. Like any business, you want your business card to be noticed, so make it as interesting as possible. Business cards are a cheap and effective way to get your Web site name out there.

Use Personalized Stationery

Although it is unlikely that you will need to have business stationery printed as an affiliate marketer, it is a good marketing strategy to include your URL on any and all letters you write. It's a simple process to set up a letterhead template in any word processing software. As long as you know the basics of word processing, you can include your logo and URL by inserting the image into your word document.

Another strategy is to include your details in your return address:

My Company Name

68 Someplace Avenue

Anywhere, State

USA 12345

(444) 555-2222

http://myURL.com

Advertise on Your Car

No doubt you have seen many cars plastered with dot-com decals, and you've made a mental note to check out the Web site when you got home or to your office. If you are like most of us, you will have forgotten the URL within a few minutes. However, if you do a lot of driving, people will get to recognize your car and its decal, and you may draw some publicity.

Use Classified Ads

Advertise your site in the classified section of local and regional newspapers. Do a small test first to see whether the return on investment will be worthwhile. Local and regional Web sites that offer a service are more likely to benefit from classified ads.

Become a Speaker

Local community, social, and charity groups are always on the look-out for new and interesting speakers, so search your local newspapers and the Yellow Pages for groups in your area that may be interested in what you have to say.

If you have a Web site about organic gardening, look for gardening clubs in your area and offer to speak about your special methods for growing prize-winning radishes. Remember to do up an information sheet to hand out at your speaking engagement so that your Web site address is readily available to the participants.

Advertise in Trade Publications

The cost to advertise in a trade publication or journal can be prohibitive if you are starting a home-based affiliate marketing business on a budget. But it might still be worth your consideration. TradePub. com (http://netprofitstoday.tradepub.com) offers free magazine trials in the following subject areas:

- Biopharmaceutical
- Business/Finance
- Computers
- Construction
- Education
- Engineering Design
- Farming and Agriculture

- Food and Beverage
- Government and Military
- Graphic Arts
- Health care
- Human Resources
- Industrial and Manufacturing
- Information Technology
- Insurance
- Internet
- Mechanical/Machinery
- Meetings and Travel
- Multimedia Design
- Network and Communications
- Purchasing and Procurement
- Retail Sales and Marketing
- Telecom and Wireless
- Trade and Professional Services
- Transportation and Logistics
- Utility and Energy

Browse the extensive list of trade publications by industry, title, keyword, or geographic eligibility to find the titles that best match your interests. Simply complete the application form and submit it.

Put Your URL on a Hat or T-Shirt

Print some hats or T-shirts with your URL and logo and wear them proudly. Give them away so others may do the same. There is a slight chance that someone will see and remember your site's URL when they get home to their computer.

CafePress (http://www.cafepress.com) is one of the leading online stores for helping you create personalized T-shirts, caps, pens, mugs, or just about any promotional item you can think of. Simply choose your design, upload your logo, and place your order. This company is very reasonably priced.

Sponsor an Event

Become a sponsor at a conference or charity event in your area. This is a good idea especially if the event is related to your industry. It doesn't cost a lot to have a small sign made up, and you can spend a few dollars on promotional products to hand out to participants. Every time they use your pen or mouse pad, your Web site name is going to be in their face.

Tell Your Friends and Family

While telling your friends and family rates a 1 out of 10 in marketing terms, more often than not it ranks first in the ego-boosting department. By all means, share your accomplishments with your friends and family. With any luck, they will pass on information about you.

Generate Word-of-Mouth Referrals

Happy customers spreading the word about your site is always a good thing. A referral from a satisfied customer places the people getting the referral halfway into the buying process by the time they get to your site.

MARKETING STRATEGIES TO AVOID

In your quest to become the best affiliate marketer you can be, you may discover sites and services that offer to help you increase your traffic through link trading or FFA (free-for-all) pages. Neither of these efforts is worth pursuing for the reasons discussed below.

Link Trading

Link trading, link exchange, or reciprocal linking is a Web promotion strategy used by webmasters and site owners to increase link popularity as well as increase qualified traffic to their sites. Page rank in search engines is influenced by the link popularity of your site. The numbers of sites that link to yours, as well as the popularity of those sites, determine link popularity. This is a relatively important factor as far as search engine placement is concerned.

You have probably seen sites with pages labeled "links" or "resources." The webmasters of these sites have listed links to their link trade partners, and the other webmasters have reciprocated by doing likewise on their sites. Links "in" to your page from another site should include your site's name or primary keyword in the link, for greater popularity.

Link popularity is improved when sites with a high page rank link to your site. A link from a site with a topic related to yours is more valuable than a link from an unrelated site. Your link popularity can actually be diminished if you trade links with sites that do not complement yours or that have low page ranks or poor traffic numbers.

A links page is an invitation for your visitors to leave your site without buying anything. Basically you are asking your visitors to go and buy at your competitors' sites.

Before pay-per-click came on the scene, link trading and links directories were all the rage. You can spend hours, if not days, writing and sending e-mails to complementary sites asking for link trades. In most cases, the reciprocating Web site or link directory will offer you a link in exchange for placing its graphic on your site. Some will go so far as to insist that you place their graphic on your homepage. You will still see many sites on which the bottom half of the page is a blinking mass (mess) of reciprocal links graphics to links directories. Do not mistake links directories for real directories like the Online Directory Project (ODP; DMOZ.org). The ODP does not require a reciprocal link to get your site listed, whereas the links sites are in the business of trading links.

In addition, the individual site owners do not benefit from these trades. Their site can't be located amidst the thousands of other affiliate sites listed in the directory. Generally, the directory owners are also an affiliate of all the same programs that you are, and you can be sure that their affiliate links are encoded in the banners at the top, middle, and bottom of their pages. Don't forget the buttons on the side, or the "superior" listings on their site.

Every link that leaves your site should generate revenue. There are only a few circumstances in which adding an unprofitable link to your site is warranted. Here's one example: When I started my Internet dating review site, Internet dating was in its infancy. People were afraid to try it, and horror stories about dates gone bad were numerous. To counter the bad press, I directed my visitors to Whoishe.com, one of the first online sites specializing in background checks. Whoishe. com did not, and still does not have an affiliate program, so I did not earn a commission for the referral if my visitors bought its product.

My rationale for posting the "leaky" (noncommission-paying) link to Whoishe.com was as a good-faith gesture that would instill confidence in visitors who wanted to buy an online dating service membership but also wanted to make sure they were protected. The only time you should put up a nonaffiliate link is if you consider the other site's information absolutely integral to your own. But keep looking for affiliate program products to replace that leaky link as soon as possible.

Free-for-All Links Pages

In your quest for traffic, you will probably come across "free for all," or FFA sites. The FFA promise looks good: "Submit your URL to have your site appear on thousands of pages across our Network." Webmasters then post their URLs on the FFA sites with the hope of generating traffic to their site. However, FFAs are nothing more than rotating lists of links. When you post to an FFA site, you are offered only one line or a couple of hundred characters to describe your site. Therefore, your link will probably never be seen by surfers.

Each and every time a site is submitted, the FFA site owner sends a confirmation e-mail to the contact address provided by the listing webmaster, which is the real purpose of the FFA site. FFA owners collect e-mail addresses so they can send out their advertising messages. They already know that you, the listing webmaster, are interested in getting traffic to your Web site, so they target their message in that direction. In most cases, the FFA site owner will then offer to sell you a service that promises to submit your site to thousands more FFA posting sites and search engines—"all for the low, low price of $59." In return, you will receive thousands more confirmation e-mails from all those other FFA site owners.

Go ahead; give it a try, if you like. Just be sure you do not use your best e-mail address. The super affiliate tip illustrates a warning to that effect that was posted on one FFA site.

SUPER AFFILIATE TIP

Warning! Do NOT use your primary e-mail address for this posting—you will receive many confirmation e-mails, and be added to many e-mail lists (you will be posting to the entire network!). We suggest using a "backup" e-mail address, or a spare free e-mail address for posting, so you will not affect your daily e-mail use.

Banner Exchange Networks

As the name implies, a banner exchange allows you to display your advertising banners on member Web sites in exchange for allowing them to display their banner on your Web site. But there is a catch. You must display two banners on your site so just one of your banners will be displayed on another member's Web site. What happens to the other 50 percent? The 50 percent would be used by the banner exchange service to display its own advertising.

There are five major drawbacks to the banner exchange scheme for traffic generation:

1. Banner exchanges do not generate significant traffic.
2. You have no control over the appearance of the other members' banners.
3. You end up with unrelated material appearing on your site.
4. Banners suck up good bandwidth and slow your pages down.

5. Banners rarely get clicked on, and their conversion rates are terrible.

Startpage or Homepage Traffic Networks

If every hit counts, then you might want to consider startpage networks as a way to get free traffic to your site. Here is a quick description of how a startpage network operates:

- Sign up and enter some basic information about the page that you want to promote.
- Set the code the network provides as your homepage or the page that opens when you start your browser.
- You then earn hits each time you open your browser window. You will earn more hits if your friends sign up through your link and open their browsers.
- The more hits you have, the more times your site will show up in other members' browsers.
- Your links are displayed all over the network, which consists of thousands of other webmasters and thousands of other sites like yours. Specifically, your links are displayed when other network users open their Web browser and when visitors leave their Web site(s) via an exit pop-under window.

(To see an example of a startpage network, visit TrafficSwarm.com.)

Refer-a-Friend Scripts

You probably have seen refer-a-friend scripts on sites you have visited. You enter both your name and e-mail address, as well as those of a number of your friends. Hit the Submit button, and a message gets sent to all those friends telling them what a great site you just found. These scripts are ineffective and not worth the time and energy it takes to load them onto your site.

SUPER AFFILIATE TIP

Use pay-per-click advertising to get the ball rolling. Then start writing. Write articles and more articles. Put them on your Web site and in your newsletter, and send them to other e-zine publishers and article directories. Think income and profit using the tools in this chapter to help you achieve both.

11

Adding It All Up

It feels great to pick up commission checks from your mailbox and deposit them in the bank on a regular basis. Unfortunately, alongside those checks you will find credit card statements and other bills for your business expenses. To stay on top of your balance sheet and make sure your affiliate marketing business stays in the black; you must pay attention to a number of different statistics. To learn exactly how well your business is doing and track its trends, you will need your Web site statistics and affiliate sales figures. Once you have collected and recorded all the relevant data, the numbers then get crunched and analyzed. In the final analysis you will learn exactly where your site is and in which direction it appears to be headed.

STATISTICS TRACKING

Before you start recording and analyzing data, you need to know what statistics you are trying to calculate, and why. Here are the four questions that you want answered during your research.

1. *What percentage of my visitors become customers?* This percentage is known as the *visitor-to-customer conversion rate,* or simply, your *conversion rate.* When webmasters speak of their conversions or say something like, "That program converts at 1.5 percent," they are talking about their visitor-to-customer conversion rate. This is probably the most important number you will ever deal with in your affiliate business. It tells you exactly how effectively you convince your visitors to buy your affiliate merchants' products. Average conversion ratios for affiliates range between 0.5 and 1.5 percent. Super Affiliates often convert their traffic at much higher percentages. In the following example, let's say your site receives 30,000 visitors in a month, and 375 of those visitors became new customers. Here is the formula:

   Conversion rate = Number of new sales divided by the number of unique visitors. (Using our numbers from above, 375 new sales/30,000 unique visitors is a conversion rate of 1.25%.

2. *What is the conversion rate for each affiliate program?* This calculation is similar to the one above. The only difference is that we use the commission and traffic statistics gathered from the individual affiliate programs, instead of totals for the site. Knowing how conversion

rates compare between programs is useful when deciding how to direct your promotional efforts. For example, if you discover that program A converts at 2 percent and that program B converts at 2.5 percent, it might be wise to spend more time and effort to promote program B! Here is the formula:

Program conversion rate = Number of new sales divided by number of unique visitors sent to affiliate site × 100. [For example, 375 (new sales)/30,000 (unique visitors) × 100 = 1.25%)

3. *How much is each visitor worth?*   Understanding how much your site earns per visitor will help you determine how much you can spend on advertising to acquire new customers. To learn how much revenue you earn per visitor, you need to know your affiliate commission amounts. Collect this information from each one of your affiliate merchant partners at the end of the month. Recording the amount of commission you expect from each merchant also makes it easier for you to see if amounts are correct when your checks arrive. Here is the formula:

Revenue per visitor = Commission earned divided by number of unique visitors (For example, $7,000 commission/30,000 uniques = $0.23 gross revenue per visitor.)

4. *How much does each visitor cost?*   This calculation determines your cost per visitor. To get your net revenue per visitor, simply subtract the results of this calculation from your revenue per visitor. For example, if you spent

$2,500 in advertising and sent 30,000 unique visitors to the merchant's site, your cost per visitor is $0.083 per visitor. So, by subtracting your cost per visitor ($0.083) from your revenue per visitor ($0.23), you end up with $0.147 net revenue per visitor. (Of course, a much easier calculation would be to subtract your expenses from your income.)

COLLECTING DATA

Each time a surfer requests one of your Web pages, all the details and files associated with that page are recorded in what is called the *server log*, which is stored on your host's server. To access this information, your host may provide full Web site statistics reporting or just the raw logs. If all you get is raw server logs, then you will probably want to use log analyzer software, because raw logs are very difficult to make sense of.

Here is some of the information you can derive from analyzing your Web site's server logs:

- Traffic data including number of unique visitors, number of visits, pages viewed, hits, bytes. These numbers will be broken down on a monthly, daily, and hourly basis.
- Number of visitors by country of origin.
- Numbers of spider/robot visits.
- Traffic source Internet protocol addresses.
- The number of times each page on your site was viewed.
- Which pages are used as entry and exit pages.
- The number and percentage of hits by file type.

- The number and percentage of hits by browser type.
- The number and percentage of hits by operating system type.
- Whether visits originated from bookmarks, search engine, newsgroup, or links from external sites (other than search engines).

Most good Web hosts give you access to your server logs. If you do not know how to find your server logs, consult your host's help files or contact the host and ask.

In addition to collecting information about your site's traffic, you will need to collect information about each of the affiliate program products that you sell on your site. You should already be checking your sales and commission information on a regular basis. In addition to number of sales and amount of commission earned, now you will also need to determine the number of unique visitors you send to the merchant's site. If the statistics about the product that you sell are found through an affiliate network, like Commission Junction, be sure you gather information about the individual product and not your collective Commission Junction statistics.

RECORDING DATA

Excel is one of the simplest and most economical programs to use to compile and record your site's financial performance data. It works well because once you have input formulas to calculate monthly totals, increases and declines, and conversion rates, you never have to do that math again. After that, you simply enter the raw data, and the spreadsheet does the calculations. You may use any spreadsheet you are comfortable with, or you might prefer to use a calculator to do the math instead. It is up to you.

Web Site Traffic

The first step is to record your Web site statistics. Input the total number of unique visitors to the site and calculate the average number of unique visitors per day and per month, as well as the increase or decrease from the previous month. To make these calculations accurate and fair, divide the number of unique visitors by the number of days in the month to arrive at the averages. (If you do not do this, February might always appear to be a dismal month for sales because it's between 8 and 10 percent shorter than the other months of the year.)

To calculate percentage of change from one month to another, simply divide the second month's uniques by the preceding month's uniques.

Example: Feb 27,626/Jan 23,839 = 1.16%

Individual Product Performance

Collect and record data from individual products to see how they perform from month to month. Once your Excel spreadsheet is set up with the correct formulas, this becomes as easy as inputting only three numbers:

1. Click throughs
2. Number of sales
3. Commission amounts

All the other figures are then calculated based on the numbers entered on the form.

Compare Product Performance After evaluating how individual products perform from month to month, the products are placed side by side, and their performance is compared. This makes it easy to see that product 1 is the best producer, not only in terms of commission earned but also by its conversion rate and average revenue per visitor.

Evaluate Month-to-Month Trends To track monthly trends, the total commission and traffic amounts of all products are added together, and the site's performance is compared from month to month. Total commissions and traffic for the year to date are added up, and average revenues per sale and per visitor are calculated.

Given this information, you can see whether your actual number of sales decreased or increased from month to month, whether your conversion rates went up or down, the site's overall performance, your total commission, and earnings per visitors.

Calculate Expenses Advertising costs are added and totaled separately. Then they are added to other costs, such as your hosting and Internet connection, to give the totals for the month.

Calculate Net Income Once both income and expenses are calculated, net income, or actual earnings from the site, can be determined. This is the amount left over that you can use to spend on that new Mercedes, after you pay your taxes.

Pay close attention to make sure that the programs you promote are turning a profit. Do not hesitate to drop a program if you find that the conversion rates for it are low or have suddenly dropped. The company may have made changes to its site or the affiliate program. Go and check them out.

While this may seem like a lot of work to go through to track your site's performance, it really is a worthwhile endeavor. Once all your formulas are set up on your spreadsheets and you have done the inputs a few times, you will be surprised at how simple it becomes. In fact, you may find that eventually you look forward to adding things up at the end of the month to get a clear picture of where your site stands. It is the only way to really know in which direction you have gone and in which direction you should turn to pursue a correct and worthwhile course.

SUPER AFFILIATE TIP

When calculating affiliate product performance, do *not* average out the traffic figures because February's lower traffic will usually be reflected in a similar decrease in the number of sales, so averaging out the traffic would make February look very dismal indeed!

12

Increase Your Profits

Most program management software allows merchants to set different rates for individual affiliates.

NEGOTIATE A COMMISSION INCREASE

If you find an excellent product that you know you can sell, it sometimes makes good sense to sign up for the affiliate program despite low commission rates in the hope that your performance will lead to a higher rate. You can promote the product for a few months and during that time establish a friendly working relationship with the affiliate manager.

After proving yourself as a webmaster who knows how to drive high-traffic volume and convert visitors to sales, ask the affiliate program manager to raise your commission rates. Be specific, and ask for a set dollar amount or percentage of the sale. The worst that can happen is that the manager will deny your request, in which case you may choose to drop the program or seriously restrict traffic to their site. In many cases, when valued affiliates drop programs or restrict traffic, affiliate managers quickly respond by negotiating better deals for those affiliates.

The key here is to prove your value as an affiliate first and then ask the company to acknowledge your value in monetary terms. It is called *building leverage*. The good companies will generally compensate properly, and there are enough good companies so that you do not need to deal with those that do not value your true worth. If you have proven yourself as a valuable affiliate who sends lots of traffic and generates lots of revenue, with whom merchant partners like to do business, most often they will be willing to negotiate a higher commission structure for you.

Affiliate managers often e-mail and ask me to review and list their services on my dating service review sites. When I receive these requests, I visit the sites and quickly look them over to make sure that they appear professional, attractive, and suitable for my audience.

My next step is to visit their affiliate homepage to check their commission rates and program specifications. I often find that the commission rates are too low to proceed with the affiliation. However, I do not just click away and forget their request. Regardless of whether or not I liked the program, I will respond, provided that their e-mail was personalized. If I liked the sites and the products, I tell the owners or affiliate managers that I think they have an excellent service that might be eligible for inclusion on my site, if they are willing to raise their commission rates. I then specify the minimum terms that I am willing to accept and leave the ball in their court.

Half the time, I do not hear back from them. That is okay, because it is the other half that counts. Merchants who understand that earning 50 percent of my sale is preferable to 90 percent of nothing are usually happy to accept my terms.

PROFIT FROM 404 ERROR PAGES

You have probably been surfing the Net and come across an "Error 404—Page Not Found" error hundreds of times. If visitors find them on your site, you are losing money. They see that page and either click the back button or close the browser window. That does not have to be the case, however, if you design a customized 404 error page for your site.

You can generally redirect your 404 page via your server. Make the page friendly and informative, and invite your visitors back to your site by offering them a range of alternatives. You may wish to include a special offer you have available or redirect them to one of your profitable but interesting pages. What that does is keep your visitor on your site. It also:

- Apologizes for the inconvenience.
- Offers them alternative options, all of which have affiliate links embedded.
- Takes a minute of your time to create a custom 404 error page and reduces potential commission losses.

GOOGLE CASHING

You can set up an affiliate marketing business without a Web site, using a method that has come to be known as "Google cashing" or "search arbitrage." This method is clearly explained by Chris Carpenter in his book *Google Cashing*.

Here is a brief three-point outline of how the strategy works.

1. Join an affiliate program.
2. Create a Google Adwords campaign for the product.
3. Send traffic from Google Adwords directly to the merchant's site with your affiliate link.

This strategy worked very well for thousands of affiliates until Google made changes to its Adwords program to improve the diversity of its search results. Before the changes were made, multiple affiliates promoting the same product would all send traffic to exactly the same page. A search for the Web hosting service HostGator might have returned a number of results all for HostGator. Surfers get confused when they see four, five, and more results that come up all pointing to the same Web site, and that makes Google look bad. So Google changed the rules and now only allows two ads for the same Web site to be displayed at any one time. Although affiliates may still create campaigns that send traffic to the same page, only those with the best click-through rate are displayed in the results. This policy change posed a challenge to many affiliates who either had to improve their ads click-through rates or had to drive traffic to a landing page on their site.

The change was a huge benefit to affiliates who sent their Adwords traffic to their own sites when Adwords prices decreased in most categories, because most of the Google cashers had their ads dropped from the results. Furthermore, because many also had no clue about how to build a Web site, they simply disappeared.

Even if you are the best copywriter in the world and can get your Google cashing ads displayed in the sponsored listings, there is another serious disadvantage to this method. When you send traffic directly to the merchant's site rather than your own, you lose the opportunity to build your list and profit from a relationship with your site's visitors. Once you have experience selling products from your own Web site, you may want to use the Google cashing method for testing new products and product categories. Until then, send traffic to your own site first.

DIVERSIFY YOUR INTERESTS

How would you cope if you had quit your full-time job and then your affiliate earnings suddenly dropped from $50,000 per month to $2,000 per month or from $2,000 per month to absolutely no income at all? Would you be able to cover your mortgage and auto loans? Online merchants file for bankruptcy, and the checks stop arriving. Products become obsolete or illegal, and entire markets disappear.

Affiliates who promoted only pharmaceutical products back in late 2004 saw their businesses decimated when the Drug Enforcement Administration shut down illegal online pharmacies with which the affiliates were doing business. The following two comments were posted on RXAffiliateForum.com. The first comment comes from one of the affiliates.

Subject: My Conversation with the FBI

I spoke with the Special agent in charge for the southeastern region for INTERNET pharmacies. I was told in no uncertain terms it is illegal to dispense medications without a doctor/patient relationship. The FBI, DEA, and other regulatory and enforcement agencies are investigating all websites that operate in this fashion.

In addition, there is no distinction between websites (read "affiliate websites"), Ops (Online pharmacies), and pharmacies. Just a heads up.

I have taken HUGE losses in the OP (Online Pharmacy) industry. ABC Merchant Site (name changed) owes me over $15,000! And XYZ Merchant Site (name changed) owes me over $5000!...There are people who have lost 2, 3, 4...even 5 times the amount that I have! And I have lost over $20,000! If you read through old posts on this forum, you will find TONS of people in the same boat. Some people have even taken legal action...but very few have got any money.

After those online pharmacies paid their fines, there probably was not much left in the company coffers to pay the commissions they owed.

The point is not to scare you away from affiliate marketing. The point is that there are potential problems with any business that you start, and you need to be both cautious and aware. There are thousands of merchants with affiliate programs, and tens of thousands of products in different markets from which to choose, so start choosing. Expand and diversify your product range to build a solid and healthy affiliate business!

13

Take Care of Business

Working from home in your own affiliate business is a dream come true for most people. Staying motivated each and every day, however, can be difficult when there is nobody looking over your shoulder or waiting for your weekly sales report. Motivation comes from being inspired and enthusiastic about what you are doing. There is nothing more motivating than visiting your mailbox every day to see if you have received another commission check.

Maintaining a regular routine and setting achievable goals can help keep you upbeat, even on those days when you wish you had pressed the snooze button. To keep your business on track, there are a number of tasks that need to be performed regularly. Use the following suggestions as a guideline for creating your own schedule.

DAILY TASKS

There are some tasks that you should try to accomplish once a day. That said, as your business grows and you gain more experience as an affiliate, you will discover that you may not have to check your statistics or links every day.

Check Your E-mails Regularly

Once you have your Web site up and running, you will want to sign up for regular newsletters from some of the masters of affiliate marketing. The trick is not to be fooled into signing up for every affiliate marketing newsletter. It is easy to be seduced by effective sales pitches. Merchant partners send out new offers and the occasional affiliate newsletter. The major affiliate networks like Commission Junction and LinkShare will send you a monthly newsletter notifying you of which of their merchants are offering deals for that month.

Keep your eyes open for e-mails with the subject line, "Check Your Merchant Status." Some merchants will drop you from their program if you aren't meeting their targets. It's likely you will not receive much e-mail from customers, because most of those will be directed to the merchant. However, if you do receive e-mail queries about products or services offered on your site, respond promptly with either the answer or an offer to redirect questions as appropriate. Both the customer and the merchant will recognize and appreciate your effort. Because the customer asked *you* the question, it means that she or he trusts your site and is probably planning to buy the product.

Write a Daily Blog Entry or Article

Adding a blog entry on a daily basis is a very good habit to develop. Your blog entries don't have to be complex or long-winded. They can be as simple as a couple of lines about a new product you've discovered or a funny thing that happened during your day. Consistent blogging is a way of adding regular content to your site and ensuring that your customers and the search engine spiders come back for more.

Maintain and Manage Your Subscriber Lists

You may receive "remove" requests from your newsletter subscribers via e-mail, despite the opt-out link of most autoresponders. Remove the subscriber's e-mail address from the opt-in list immediately. Justified or not, spam complaints are something you do not ever want to get.

Continually Monitor Your Site

Regularly check to ensure that your site is online. Type your URL into your browser's address bar, refresh the page, and find out at least once a day (if not more) that your site is online. Pay-per-click advertising costs add up whether your site is functional or not. If your site is down, you are paying for advertising, but no one is buying.

If that thought scares you, NetMechanic (http://netmechanic. com) is a service that will check every 15 minutes 24 hours a day to see whether your site in online. If your site is down, the service will notify you by numeric pager, alphanumeric pager, or e-mail, so you can resolve your downtime problems immediately. Check out its free trial, which will check your site every 15 minutes for 8 hours so you can see how their service works.

Regularly Check Your Links

Broken sales links are the bane of an affiliate marketer's existence. Merchants have been known to change their link structure and advise you some time later. In many cases your HTML editor will have a built-in link checker. If this is not available, use NetMechanic to check those links.

Monitor and Check Site Statistics

When you first start out, it is likely that you will want to check your stats hourly, and sometimes even more often. Once you become more familiar with the income trends, you will probably want to check your key partner sites daily to see how your business is performing. It is recommended that you check your statistics daily until you know what to expect day by day and week by week. Simply visit the statistics interface for each network and individual affiliate partner and input your total revenues to a spreadsheet you have developed. (Using Quicken will also keep you informed as to whether certain checks are overdue.)

Give Yourself Time Off

A business that involves sitting at a computer for lengthy periods of time can lead to weight gain and repetitive strain injury if you do not take proper care of yourself. Start your day in a healthy way by trying to put in some exercise before you turn on your computer in the morning. That is the best way to not get sidetracked by business interests. Every 50 minutes or so, take a 10-minute break, get up and stretch your legs, and look into the distance. You can give yourself eye strain by continually staring at a computer monitor for extended periods of time.

Plan Your Day Ahead of Time

It is very easy to get distracted in this industry by e-mails, "urgent" correspondence, and a million and one other tasks that prevent you from getting the real work done. Prioritizing is the key. At the end of each day, record in your diary the tasks that have to get done the next day in order of their priority. So when you sit down at your computer to start each day, you are ready to hit the ground running.

Do not start your day by checking your e-mails, reading newsletters, visiting news sites, or scanning blogs. Begin with the first task on your list and work steadily at it for at least 50 minutes. Only when you have completed the tasks that you have established as a priority should you go back and take care of your e-mails, newsletters, and other tasks. If there is a task that did not get completed from the prior day, make it first priority for the next day.

WEEKLY TASKS

Stay abreast of your industry through research, and pass what you learn on to your visitors and newletter subscribers on a weekly basis.

Create New Content

Search engine spiders love fresh content—so give it to them. Add new content to your site every week to keep it fresh. Not only will fresh content bring the search engine spiders, but it will also encourage your visitors to keep coming back to your site.

Research, Write, and Publish Your Newsletter

Aim to publish your newsletter not less than once a week. Many other Internet marketers recommend publishing more frequently, and some report that their best results come from publishing once a day. You want to constantly remind your subscribers that you are still there and in business, and the more you communicate with them, the more they will learn to trust you and keep coming back to your Web site for more. By using RSS feeds (see Chapter 10), you can keep up to date with trends and changes in your market, and regular news feeds give you fodder for your newsletter content.

Perform Regular Keyword Searches

Always be on the lookout for new keywords and keyword phrases to add to your pay-per-click advertising campaigns. Jot down your ideas, and then add them to the advertisement you submit to Yahoo! Search Marketing, Miva, and other campaigns on a weekly basis.

Research, Research, Research

Spend time every week reviewing and researching the news in your industry, as well as Internet marketing news. Learning about new methods and tools for doing business can save you time and money down the road. Set aside a couple of hours one afternoon each week—Friday afternoon is always a good time to devote to research and reading.

Check on Your Competition

Your aim is to become an industry leader, not a follower, but occasionally your competitors will come upon an idea or product that is new and potentially profitable. That is why it is important to keep an eye on what your competition is doing. You can always try to stay one step ahead.

MONTHLY TASKS

Following are things you should be taking care of once a month:

- Complete your monthly traffic and affiliate sales statistics to determine visitor value.

- Tally your income and expenses to stay on top of your overall business picture.
- Enter data into your spreadsheets to see which direction your traffic and sales conversions are moving.

QUARTERLY TASKS

At least once every three months you should be working on launching a new site. Diversification is the best way to hedge your bets against significant market upheavals. Events in recent years such as those that took place on September 11, 2001, the war in Iraq, and the outbreak of SARS have affected businesses online and off. When your business is diversified, you will see that while some sales plummet during times of crisis, others will increase.

For example, despite fears in the online dating industry of very poor sales following the events of 9/11 in New York, most of the top dating Web sites reported that sales of dating service memberships actually increased. (Perhaps this could be perceived as peoples' need to connect and share their feelings about this horrific tragedy with others.)

At any rate, do not put all your eggs in one basket. Always be on the lookout for profitable markets and great merchants with affiliate programs. Plan to launch a new affiliate site at least once every quarter to protect yourself against the vagaries of an increasingly unstable market.

YEARLY TASKS

Get ready for the IRS and the new year by completing these yearly tasks.

Complete Year-End Statistics and Taxes

You must be sure that you complete year-end statistics and taxes. Whether you operate as a sole proprietor or incorporate your business, you will need to prepare taxes. You will also want to complete an end-of-year statistical summary to assess how your Web sites performed, where you need to work harder, and where you want to go next.

Set Goals for the Year Ahead

Although it is good business practice to set daily, weekly, and monthly goals, you will find it even more helpful to set annual financial goals. Create a master plan to execute all of the goals on a yearly basis. (It would be difficult to find a highly successful Webpreneur who does not have a list of goals—both short and long term.)

At the end of each year, assess the long-term goals you made for yourself and tick off those you have achieved. Look at the goals you haven't yet achieved, and either give them a new completion date or ask yourself honestly what happened that prevented you from meeting those goals. Reward yourself for those goals you have achieved, and then do an honest appraisal of why you didn't achieve some of the goals you had set. This is the time to look at your business plan and make adjustments so that at the same time next year you can put a big red checkmark next to those goals.

14

Avoid the Pitfalls

To err is human, so don't be afraid to make mistakes. Mistakes are merely lessons from which we can learn, and many mistakes can easily be avoided when we learn from the mistakes of others.

20 MISTAKES TO AVOID AS AN AFFILIATE

As an affiliate, you should try to avoid making the following 20 mistakes:

1. *Spamming.* *Spam* is unsolicited e-mail. As well as not asking to receive it, recipients have every right to contact your ISP or the merchant involved in the offer, both of whom will likely terminate their association with you immediately. (Watch out for unrealistic e-mail promotions that offer deals for leads such as "$99.95 for 500,000

e-mails." Sending e-mail to those addresses is spamming—pure and simple.)

2. *Not doing market research.* Trying to sell products that people do not want is a futile endeavor. Test the waters before you invest time and money in a new project.

3. *Failing to plan.* As the old saying goes, "Fail to plan, plan to fail." Without a map, a journey into unknown territory takes much longer, costs more money, and may get you lost. Simplify your project by having a well-developed plan.

4. *Posting ads on forums.* Forums and discussion boards are excellent sources of valuable information about Internet and affiliate marketing. Akin to spamming, posting advertising on message boards can get the poster banned. Avoid acting in ways that upset the forum or message board owners and administrators.

5. *Overusing merchant ad copy.* Successful affiliates set themselves apart from other affiliates that are promoting the same products by offering something fresh and new. When you use advertising copy prepared by the merchants, you are not giving your visitors any new information.

6. *Infringing on copyrights.* Treat others' work with respect. How would you feel if you found an exact copy of your site on someone else's domain? Always ask permission to use graphic images or text found on another site.

7. *Submitting to FFAs.* There are drawbacks to submitting sites to free-for-all (FFA) sites. (FFA sites are Web sites that contain a collection of jumbled links to other sites

and that serve no useful purpose.) Your site will never get seen, so posting is a waste of time. Worse, because most FFAs have low rankings, your site's rankings will drop by association.

8. *Shouting.* Other than using capital letters to emphasize a few words within an e-mail or on a Web page, refrain from using caps. Using all capital letters in text or correspondence is symbolic of shouting, and shouting at people just makes them leave.

9. *Not responding to visitor e-mails.* If a visitor e-mails a question to an affiliate and that affiliate does not reply in a timely manner, the visitor will go elsewhere for an answer and will become someone else's customer.

10. *Overusing pop-ups.* Getting hit by multiple pop-ups is annoying. Many surfers will choose to close their browsers completely rather than click x 20 times. No browser—no sale. In any case, many surfers choose to use pop-up blockers these days, so your pop-ups become useless.

11. *Using free-hosts and e-mail accounts.* Using free hosts and e-mail accounts looks cheesy and unprofessional. How confident do you feel buying products from someone who will not pay $9.95 to register a domain?

12. *Not having an opt-in newsletter.* Without an opt-in list, your visitors come, and then they go. You have no way to contact them again. Those who sign up to receive your newsletters or ads are telling you that they are interested in the products you offer. That is like having a license to print money.

13. *Keeping poor records.* Did that check from XYZ Company arrive? Was the amount correct? If your record keeping is less than accurate, you might never know. Do not get cheated—keep track of your business activities.

14. *Building a mall.* A mall site is best used as a central hub to send visitors to other Web sites. Mall sites do not get much search engine traffic, and they do not convert to sales. Highly focused theme sites attract traffic *and* sales.

15. *Out-of-date advertising.* Prices change all the time. With the exception of current price quotes placed in your newsletter, product prices do not belong on your site. Banners or text links that expire are guaranteed to eventually send your visitor to a broken link or show a broken graphic on your page. Time-sensitive advertising is best used only in e-mail advertising campaigns.

16. *Using leaky links.* Do you take money out of your wallet and throw it away? That is exactly what you are doing when you pay for traffic and then send visitors to another site through anything other than affiliate links.

17. *Placing affiliate links on the homepage.* Putting affiliate links on your homepage is like showing visitors in the front door and immediately out the back. Give them a chance to browse, sign up for your newsletter, and decide that they'd like to come back to your place before introducing them to your very attractive friends.

18. *Trying to do it all.* Do not try to be a jack-of-all-trades and master of none. Hire an expert when required and save yourself time and money.

19. *Failing to act.*   What isn't started does not get done. It is true that the first step is the hardest, but if you never act, you will never enjoy the incredible rewards waiting for you.

20. *Giving up.*   Just as Rome wasn't built in a day, you should not expect overnight riches from the Net. Enjoy the process. Know that some days will be more challenging than others, and keep at it. Persistence is the single most important factor in determining success online or off. Be persistent and be successful.

POTENTIAL PROBLEMS WITH PROGRAMS

Stuff happens. From time to time you will encounter difficulties with a program. Here are some examples of that "stuff" that can happen and some suggestions on how to avoid problems.

Application Is Rejected

It can be disappointing to receive an e-mail like the one shown in Figure 14.1

To avoid receiving such a letter, be sure to read and understand all the ins and outs of the program you wish to join. Then dot your i's and cross your t's when submitting your application.

Of course, even affiliate managers make mistakes occasionally. If you receive a letter like the one shown in Figure 14.1 and believe it was in error, contact the affiliate program manager and politely ask why your site was rejected. Be sure to state why you feel your site is a good match for the program.

Figure 14.1   Rejection E-Mail

Dear (affiliate marketer),

Thank you for applying to XYZ Services.

We regret to inform you that your application was not approved for this program. This is not intended as disapproval of the quality or value of your Web site. Each advertiser determines how many and what types of publishers they will accept in their program for various reasons. You are welcome to apply to other advertiser programs in the network at any time. We apologize for any inconvenience this may cause you.

For assistance, please use the "Support" drop-down menu at the top of this page.

Best regards,
XYZ Network

Affiliation Is Terminated

Not getting accepted into an affiliate program, for whatever reason, is hard to take; but getting terminated once you are in is even worse. Figure 14.2 is an example of a termination letter. (Just so you know what one looks like. If you follow my suggestions in this book you'll never get one.)

Program termination happens when you join an affiliate program before you are ready to write a product review or simply do not send the merchant enough traffic. To avoid having this happen to you, make sure that your site is online and complete before applying to programs. Better still, before you apply to a program, write

Figure 14.2 Termination Letter

Dear (affiliate marketer),

With the goal of improving our focus on key publisher relationships, we recently reviewed all of our existing CJ publisher accounts to determine who was actively engaged in promoting and driving qualified sales to XYZAffiliateProgram.

You are receiving this e-mail because your account was identified as one that is either not active or driving clicks but no sales over the past year.

For this reason, we will be terminating our relationship with you.

Because of the volume of sites in our program, it is possible that your account was selected for termination in error. We encourage you to contact us if you think that this is the case, or if you have a distinct strategy you plan to employ to activate XYZAffiliateProgram in your program. Please include your affiliate ID, the site from which you are linking to us, and any other information that you think we should be aware of.

Sincerely,

Your XYZAffiliateProgram Team

---

descriptions and endorsements for the products you plan to promote and post the review to your site. Send the manager the link to your product review page. Provided that the quality of your review is good, you will have no problem getting into the program—and your affiliation will not be terminated for lack of effort. Once you're accepted, all you will have to do is add your links and use pay-per-click to drive traffic to your site right away.

Know When to Terminate Your Affiliation

Some affiliations weren't meant to be, or they turn sour. When that happens, it is time to drop the program and move on to greener, more lucrative pastures. The following five scenarios warrant dropping an affiliate program.

1. The Program Fails to Pay What You Are Owed Although failure to pay is a rare occurrence, it is important to keep track of what you are owed and when you expect to receive payment.

- If you fail to receive a check within two weeks of its expected arrival, first make a print screen image of the affiliate interface that shows your earnings.
- Next, contact the affiliate manager, explain the situation, and ask when you can expect to receive the payment.
- If the check again fails to arrive by the stated date, contact the affiliate manager again and request an immediate payment via PayPal.
- Take down all your links at this point and visit one of the popular affiliate forums to report the issue and get feedback from other affiliates on their experience with the company.

You may end up chalking up a loss, but in most cases the situation will be resolved amicably.

2. The Program Fails to Compensate for Server or Site Downtime Sites go down from time to time. However, for affiliates who pay to send traffic to those sites, there is a certain protocol most good affiliate merchants follow. First they tell their affiliates about the outage immediately and then they compensate for lost revenue on the basis of past performance. (Do not do business with any company that simply advises its affiliates of an outage and then fails to compensate appropriately.)

3. Commission Payments Are Received Later than Expected If your commission payments are consistently slow to arrive, it may be best to drop the program. Slow payments may be an indicator that the company is unstable and may ultimately end up not paying you at all.

4. You Receive Frequent or Regular Complaints about the Product Repeated complaints from customers about a specific product, service, or company are one of the best reasons to drop a program. If you have a good relationship with the affiliate program manager, pass your visitors' comments along. Ask the manager to let you know when the problem will be corrected. If you do not have the time or if the affiliate cannot guarantee that the problem will be resolved, drop the program.

5. You Receive Spam to the E-Mail Address Set Up for a Particular Program Although it may seem incredible that an affiliate program manager would spam his or her own affiliates, it does happen. One way to find out who is sending you spam is to create individual e-mail addresses for each of the programs that you join.

Example: You sign up to promote XYZAffiliateProgram.com's product and create the address XYZAffiliateProgram@mydomain. com. If you start receiving spam to that address, notify the manager that your address for that program was spammed. In some cases, an employee of the program or network will steal and sell affiliates' addresses for his or her own benefit. The best case scenario is that the manager ferrets out and fires the rogue employee for breaking the law. However, if the manager cannot explain how or why spam was sent to that address, drop the program.

6. The Affiliate Manager Expects You to Jump on Command Some affiliate managers seem not to appreciate that affiliates are busy people. Some affiliates are partnered with hundreds of programs. Others enjoy regular vacations away from their computers. They therefore cannot always be expected to respond immediately to every request they receive. Figure 14.3 shows excerpts from a real e-mail that was sent to affiliates on August 28, with the subject line: "URGENT: Change your links on August 29!"

Figure 14.3   Expectation of Immediate Response

We're about to reveal some very exciting changes this week that will make it easier than ever for you to earn commissions with us! To take advantage of these changes, you must change all the (name of program) links on your site on August 29 . . .

You *MUST* change your banners, tiles and links on August 29 . . .

We will not be able to track or compensate you for members that are generated through old links after that date . . .

Please note they (the affiliate links) will not be functional until August 29!

In effect, this company expected its affiliates to change and upload all the new links at exactly midnight on August 29. This notice was not only untimely, but it was thoughtless and inconsiderate.

PREVENT COMMISSION THEFT

Both consumers and other affiliates can and will try to rob you of your commissions. Consumers steal affiliate commissions by removing an affiliate's identification from the URL prior to clicking through to the site. Since it costs no more money to buy through the affiliate link, it is baffling that consumers would deprive an affiliate of its rightful commission—but they do. Other affiliate marketers will swap your affiliate ID for their own affiliate ID to get the commission when they buy the product. In effect, they are discounting their own purchase.

Responsible merchants have systems in place to prevent this type of commission theft. However, some merchants do nothing to prevent affiliate commission theft, so it is up to you as an affiliate to protect your commissions. To beat the cheaters, use "Affiliate Link Cloaker" software, which is available at AfiliateLinkCloaker.com. The software is easy to use. You input the affiliate link that you want to hide and name and save an HTML page (i.e., cloaker.html). Then upload it to your server.

IDENTIFY POTENTIAL CONTENT THEFT

It is a good idea to search occasionally on Google for articles you have written to see how they have been published on other webmasters' sites. From time to time, you will stumble across a webmaster who has published your material on his or her site without including the link to your site, which amounts to taking something for nothing, otherwise known as theft. When that happens and if contact information is available on the site in question, contact the webmaster and politely ask that the URL to your site be included or that the article be removed. Most webmasters will comply with your request. For those who do not, you may just have to chalk up the experience to the cost of doing business.

GET UNFAIR PPC COMPETITORS REMOVED

Webmasters that advertise irrelevant keyword terms at pay-per-click search engines push bid prices up unfairly. For example, let's say that an advertiser under the keyword "running shoe" is bidding 30 cents to hold the top spot. If you too are selling running shoes and want to hold the first position, you would have to pay 31 cents. However, if the site currently in the top spot does not in fact sell running shoes, you and other advertisers should not have to compete with that site.

If you discover completely irrelevant site advertising in the paid listings at any one of the pay-per-click search engines, take the time to drop the editors a note about your findings. Yahoo! Search Marketing, Google, and other pay-per-click search engines all have advertiser guidelines that are very stringent about relevancy. You therefore should have no problem getting this site removed from the sponsored listings when you contact the relevant service. Not only will you save money by writing that note, but you will also help save Internet surfers time when they do not have to visit useless and irrelevant sites.

SUPER AFFILIATE TIP

Don't hesitate to drop a program in any of the situations discussed here. Hanging onto a merchant partnership that does not respect its affiliates will end up costing you time and money.

15

Final Words

SUPER AFFILIATE BUSINESS STRATEGIES

As you grow your affiliate marketing business, you will begin to increasingly see offers for software and education packages that promise to help you get rich quick or build 3,000 Web sites this weekend. The vast majority of these get-rich-quick promises are gray hat or black hat schemes that use dubious tricks that can kill your business in the blink of an eye. Both gray and black hats use dubious and often frowned-upon strategies that can get your site banned by the search engines and put you out of favor with your affiliated merchants. Too many webmasters who relied solely on search engine traffic have returned to full-time salaried employment, working for someone else.

Following are six ways in which the strategies presented in this book differ from the gray-hat approach to affiliate sites.

1. *Profit from what you know.*   Putting profit potential first is a sure recipe for failure, especially when you are just starting out. Building your business around a topic about which you are passionate or knowledgeable and one that has huge profit potential should form the foundation of your business strategy. The added benefit is that you will enjoy yourself. Time spent having fun is not work. It feels like play.

2. *Show respect for visitors.*   Successful affiliates build Web sites for people, not search engines. To satisfy your customers' needs and wants and to gain their respect and trust, build sites with real content such as product endorsements, quality articles, and honest reviews.

3. *Fewer sites; better content.*   Building dozens of poor-quality sites seems more like an assembly-line job than a business. Rather than developing huge numbers of substandard sites, develop a lucrative, affiliate business around high-quality content sites that entice a large number of visitors.

4. *Use multiple marketing methods.*   Super Affiliates never need to worry that their traffic or income will suddenly disappear. There is a variety of ways to guarantee that your sites always receive a flow of traffic. Therefore, if one method of traffic delivery slows down or fails, many more are in place to sustain or even boost your income.

5. *Build community.*   Super Affiliates build communities to interact with their visitors through newsletters, blogs, and forums. As your visitors get to know and trust you, your visitor-to-customer conversion rate increases.

6. *Branding.* Community interaction and knowledge "brands" you as a trusted source of valuable information. Your income increases with new and repeat visitors as surfers recognize and trust you as an expert in your chosen area.

Like any other legitimate business, affiliate marketing takes time, patience, and effort. Use the techniques discussed here to build a solid business and reputation that will serve you well into the future.

SUPER AFFILIATE CHARACTERISTICS

Following are the predominant factors that set Super Affiliates apart from their less productive counterparts.

- *Super Affiliates treat affiliate marketing as a business.* They invest time, money, and effort in their business. They are enthusiastic, determined, and persistent. (They do not slap together a site with a couple of banner ads.)
- *Super Affiliates are focused.* They find a niche with a huge market. They research, understand, and sell to that market.
- *Super Affiliates are super communicators.* They know and understand their merchants' products, and they know how to sell the benefits of those products to their visitors.
- *Super Affiliates grow their businesses.* After building one successful affiliate site, they look for opportunities to develop new streams of income with more affiliate programs.
- *Super Affiliates are constantly learning.* They stay current

with industry trends in order to stay on top of what they need to know about how to conduct their business successfully.

Do what it takes to become a Super Affiliate, and you, too, will make a fortune selling other people's stuff online.

I wish you the very best in your affiliate marketing adventures!

Glossary

The Internet brings with it a language all its own. This glossary explains the meaning of the terms most commonly used.

A

Above the Fold: Once a Web page has loaded, the part that is visible is said to be "above the fold."

Adware: Also known as "spyware," a program hidden within free downloaded software that transmits user information via the Internet to advertisers.

Affiliate: A Web site owner who promotes a merchant's products and/or services and earns a commission for referring clicks, leads, or sales.

Affiliate Agreement: Terms that govern the relationship between a merchant and an affiliate.

Affiliate Program: Any arrangement through which a merchant pays a commission to an affiliate for generating clicks, leads, or sales from links located on the affiliate's site. Also known as associate, partner, referral, and revenue sharing programs.

Affiliate Program Directory: Information about a collection of affiliate programs. May include information about commission rate, number of affiliates, and commission structure.

Affiliate Program Manager: The person responsible for administering an affiliate program. Duties usually include maintaining regular contact with affiliates, program marketing, and responding to queries about the program.

Affiliate Solution Provider: Company that provides the software and services to administer an affiliate program.

Affiliate URL or Link: Special code in a graphic or text link that identifies a visitor as having arrived from a specific affiliate site.

Applet: A small javascript program embedded in an HTML page.

Associate: Synonym for affiliate.

Autoresponder: An e-mail robot that sends replies automatically, without human intervention. For example, if you had a page of marketing information, you could ask prospects to send e-mail to "info@yourname.com," the address of your autoresponder. The autoresponder will automatically e-mail the person your information document. Many autoresponders will, at the same time, send an e-mail to you, listing the requester's address and the document requested. This is an important tool for conducting online commerce.

B

Bandwidth: The number of bits-per-second sent through a connection. A full page of text is about 16,000 bits.

Banner Ad: Advertising in the form of a graphic image.

Bit (*B*inary Dig*it*):   The smallest unit of computerized data. It is a single digit number, either a 1 or a 0.

Bits per Second (bps):   A measurement of how fast data are moved from one place to another. A 56.6 modem can move 56,600 bits per second, but usually doesn't.

Blog: Taken from "We*b log*," a blog is basically a journal that is available on the Web. The act of updating a blog is referred to as "blogging," and those who keep blogs are known as "bloggers."

Browser: A program that allows you to access and read hypertext documents on the World Wide Web. An example is Internet Explorer (IE).

C

CGI (Common Gateway Interface):   Programs that perform certain functions in connection with your HTML documents. For example, a common CGI script is a counter, which keeps track of the number of people who access your homepage. Many CGI scripts are available for free use on the World Wide Web. Always check with your webmaster before using a new CGI script. You can often see that a CGI script is being used when you see "cgi-bin" in the URL.

CGIi-bin: A directory on a Web server in which CGI programs are stored.

Chargeback: An incomplete or invalid sales transaction that results in an affiliate commission deduction.

Click-Through: When a user clicks on a link and arrives at a Web site.

Click-Through Ratio (CTR):   Percentage of visitors who click through to a merchant's Web site.

Client: A software program used to contact and obtain data from a software program on another computer. For example, the e-mail program Eudora is an e-mail client.

Cloaking: Hiding of page code content.

Co-Branding: Situation in which affiliates are able include their own logo and/or colors on the merchant's site.

Comment Code: HTML tags used to hide text and code scripting from browsers.

Commission: Also known as a bounty or referral fee, the income an affiliate is paid for generating a sale, lead, or click-through to a merchant's Web site.

Contextual Link: Placement of affiliate links within related text.

Conversion: When one of your visitors makes a purchase on the merchant's site, that is, converts from visitor to buyer.

Conversion Rate: The percentage of visits to a site that converts to a sale; for example, if one person in every hundred visitors to your site makes a purchase, then your conversion rate is 1:100 or 1 percent.

Cookie: A piece of information sent by a Web server to a Web browser that the browser software is expected to save and to send back to the server whenever the browser makes additional requests from the server. You may set your browser to either accept or not accept cookies. Cookies can contain user preferences, log-in or registration information, and/or "shopping cart" information. When a cookied browser sends a request to a server, the server uses the information to return customized information.

Cost-per-Acquisition (CPA):   The amount you pay to acquire a customer.

Cost-per-Click (CPC):   The amount you pay when a surfer clicks on one of your listings.

Cost-per-Thousand (CPM):   The amount you pay per 1,000 impressions of a banner or button.

Creative: The promotional tools advertisers use to draw in users. Examples are text links, towers, buttons, badges, e-mail copy, pop-ups, and so forth.

Cyberspace: William Gibson coined the term in his book, *Neuromancer*. Cyberspace now describes the whole range of data available through computer networks.

D

Demographics: The physical characteristics of a population such as age, sex, marital status, family size, education, geographic location, and occupation.

Digital Subscriber Line (DSL): A very fast way to move data over phone lines.

Disclaimer: A disclaimer states the terms under which a site or work may be used and gives information relating to what the copyright owner believes to be a breach of copyright. In some cases you may wish to permit certain activities; in others you may wish to withhold all rights or require the user to apply for a license to carry out certain actions.

Domain Name: The unique name that identifies an Internet site; composed of two or more parts and separated by dots.

Doorway Page: *See* gateway page.

Download: Transfer of a file from another computer to your own.

E

E-mail: Electronic mail, a message sent to another Internet user across the Internet. An e-mail address looks like this: jimsmith@bubblee.com, where "jimsmith" is the user name (the unique identifier); "@" stands for "at," and " bubblee.com" is the name of the Internet service provider.

E-mail Link: An affiliate link to a merchant site contained in an e-mail newsletter or signature file.

E-mail Signature (Sig File): A brief message embedded at the end of every e-mail that a person sends.

EPC: Term used by the Commission Junction affiliate network; refers to the average earnings per 100 clicks. This number is calculated by taking commissions earned divided by the total number of clicks times 100.

E-zine: Short for electronic magazine.

F

File Transfer Protocol (FTP):   The most common method used for moving files between computers, servers, and Internet sites.

Fire Wall: Hardware and/or software used to separate a local area network into two or more parts for security purposes.

Flame: Derogatory comment.

Frequently Asked Questions (FAQ):   Lists of and answers to the most common questions asked on a particular subject. Generally posted to avoid having to answer the same question repeatedly.

G

Gateway: See Internet service provider.

Gateway Page: Also known as bridge pages, doorway page, entry pages, portals, or portal pages; these pages are used to improve search engine placement. Caution: Some search engines will drop a site entirely if the existence of doorway/gateway pages is detected.

Graphic Interchange Format (GIF):   An image file format suitable for simple files. A JPEG is the preferred format for storing photographs.

H

Hit: A hit is a single request from for a single item on a Web server. To load a page with five graphics would count as six hits—one for the page plus one for each of the graphics. Hits therefore are not a very good measure of traffic to a Web site.

Homepage: Your primary HTML page, the first page anyone would see in your Web site. Also called a "landing page."

Hybrid Model: A commission model that combines different payment methods.

Hype (Hyperbole):   A deliberate exaggeration for emotional effect. The addressee is not expected to have a literal understanding of the expression.

Hypertext: A hypertext document has references to other documents sprinkled throughout. If you click on one of these references, you are transferred to an entirely different document. For example, if a glossary was a hypertext document, you could click on any of the hypertext link's words and you'd instantly be transported to the definition of that word.

Hypertext Markup Language (HTML): The primary language that World Wide Web documents are created in.

I

Impression: An advertising metric that indicates how many times an advertising link is displayed.

In-house: Merchant that administers its own affiliate program.

Internet: Interconnected networks that use TCP/IP protocols.

Internet Service Provider (ISP): The company you call from your computer to gain access to the Internet.

Intranet: A company or organization's private network that uses the same type of software found on the Internet but that is only for internal use.

IP (Internet Protocol) Address: A unique number consisting of four parts separated by dots, for example, 165.115.245.2. Every machine on the Internet has a unique IP address.

J

Javascript: A programming language developed by Sun Microsystems and designed for writing programs that can be safely downloaded to your computer through the Internet and immediately run without fear of viruses or other harm to your computer or files. Javascript requires a browser compatible with java. Using small java programs, Web pages can include animations, calculators, and other features.

Joint Venture: A general partnership typically formed to undertake a particular business transaction or project rather than one intended to continue indefinitely.

K

Keyword: The search term that a user may enter at a search engine. For example, someone who wants to find a site that sells printers might enter "printer " at a search engine. "Printer" is the keyword.

Keyword Density: The ratio between the keyword being searched for and the total number of words appearing on your Web page. If your keyword occurs only once, in a page that has 20,000 words, then it has a density of 0.005 percent.

L

Lifetime Value: The total amount of money that a customer will spend with a particular company during his or her lifetime.

Link: A "clickable" object that, when clicked, will take the viewer to a particular page or place on a page, or start a new e-mail with an address that is specified.

Link Popularity: The total number of qualified Web sites linking to one particular Web site.

Local Area Network (LAN):   Computers linked together in a central location, such as a business or government organization.

M

Manual Approval: Process in which all applicants for an affiliate program are reviewed individually and manually approved.

Media Metrix: Measures traffic counts on all the Web sites on the Net. It publishes the top 50 sites in the United States, the global top 50, and the Media Metrix Top 500 Web sites.

Merchant: A business that markets and sells goods or services.

Merchant Account: A commercial bank account established by contractual agreement between a business and a bank. A merchant account enables the business to accept credit card payments from customers.

Meta Tags: Information placed in the header of an HTML page, which is not visible to site visitors.

Modulator/Demodulator (MODEM):   The card that allows your computer to connect to the phone line and communicate with other computers.

Mosaic: The first major browser program.

Multilevel Marketing (MLM):   Also known as network marketing, MLM involves the sale of products through a group of independent distributors who buy wholesale, sell retail, and sponsor other people to do the same.

Multipurpose Internet Mail Extensions (MIME):   Allow an e-mail message to contain nontext data, such as audio and video files.

N

Netscape: Makers of the Netscape Navigator browser.

Newbie: Someone who is new to the Internet.

Newsgroup: A newsgroup is a discussion that takes place online and is devoted to a particular topic. The discussion takes the form of electronic messages called "postings" that anyone with a newsreader (standard with most browsers) can post or read.

P

Pay-per-Click (PPC):   An advertising payment model in which the advertiser pays only when the advertisement is actually clicked. Also, an affiliate program in which affiliates receive a commission for each click (visitor) they refer to a merchant's Web site.

Pay-per-Lead (PPL):   A program in which affiliates receive a commission for each sales lead that they generate for a merchant's Web site. Examples include completed surveys, contest or sweepstakes entries, downloaded software demos, or free trials.

Pay-per-Sale (PPS):   Programs in which affiliates receive a commission for each sale of a product or service that they refer to a merchant's Web site.

Plug-in: A small piece of software that adds features to a larger piece of software.

Politeness Window: Most search engine spiders will not crawl an entire site in one session. Instead, they crawl a couple of pages and return after a day or two to crawl a couple more and so on until they have indexed the entire site. This is a self-imposed limit in order not to overburden a server. The time period between sessions is known as the politeness window.

Portable Document Format (PDF):   A distribution format developed by Adobe Corporation to allow electronic information to be transferred between various types of computers. The software that allows this transfer is called Acrobat.

Portal: A Web site that is intended to be used as a main point of entry to the Web. For example, MSN.com is a portal site.

Posting: A message entered into a newsgroup or message board.

Post Office Protocol (POP):   Refers to the way e-mail software such as Eudora gets mail from a mail server.

Privacy Policy: A policy designed to establish how a company collects and uses information about its customers' accounts and transactions.

Profit: The amount of money you earn from your sales. For example, if you sell 10 videos at $47 each, and each costs $10 to produce and ship, your profit would be $37 per video or $370 total.

Protocol: A method or language of communication.

Proxy Server: Computers, such as those belonging to Internet service providers, that act as agents for multiple users, resulting in many users having only one IP address.

R

Really Simple Syndication (RSS): An XML-based format for syndicated content.

Referring URL: The URL a user came from to reach your site.

Residual Earnings: Programs that pay affiliates for each sale a shopper from their sites makes at the merchant's site over the life of the customer.

Return on Advertising Spend (ROAS): The amount of revenue generated per amount spent on an advertising method.

Return on Investment (ROI): The amount derived from subtracting your net revenue from your total costs.

Revenue: Total income from your sales. For example, if you sell 50 e-books at $27 each, your revenue would be $1,350.

Robot: Any browser program not directly under human control that follows hypertext links and accesses Web pages. For example, a search engine spider is a robot.

S

Scumware: Software that contains additional features for the purpose of displaying advertisements. This software will modify Web pages from their original content to put ads on the user's computer screen. Examples of scumware propagators include Gator, Ezula, Surf+, and Imesh.

Search Term Suggestion Tool: Displays how many times a certain keyword was searched for at Yahoo! Search Marketing during a given month.

Secure Server: Allows a connection between itself and another secure server. Secured connections provide three essential things concerning online transactions: privacy, authentication, and message integrity. When viewing Web pages or posting information to a secure server, you'll notice that the "http://" that usually appears in the Web address bar changes to "https://." Also, on most Web browsers, the symbol of a closed padlock should appear somewhere in the browser's frame as an indicator that you are using a secure connection.

Server: The computer hardware that stores your homepage and sends and receives information through the World Wide Web.

Server Logs: Each time a user accesses a Web page, information is recorded on the server logs. Server logs contain information about what pages were accessed, along with the date, time, and computer's IP address. Other statistics can also be tracked, including username, browser type, previous page, and so forth.

Shockwave: Codeveloped by Netscape and Macromedia, software that allows animations and interactive programs to be embedded into HTML pages.

Sig (Signature File or Sig Line):   The author's signature at the end of an e-mail or online post. Commonly consists of an e-mail address and other contact information, very brief information about a business, and perhaps a favorite quotation or funny phrase.

Social Bookmarking: Web sites that enable you to list your favorite and most visited sites (similar to Google Favorites) except that you can invite friends and others to access and see your "bookmarked" pages. You can also tag your favorite pages using keywords to keep them in order and attract search engine spiders.

SPAM: Internet expression that refers to unsolicited commercial e-mail (UCE) or unsolicited bulk e-mail (UBE). Some people refer to this kind of communication as junk e-mail to equate it with the paper junk mail that comes through the U.S. mail. Unsolicited e-mail is e-mail that you did not request; it most often contains advertisements for services or products.

Spyware: Also known as "adware," a program hidden within free downloaded software that transmits user information via the Internet to advertisers.

SQL (structured query language):   A programming language for sending queries to databases.

SSL (secure sockets layer):   A protocol used to enable encrypted, authenticated communications across the Internet. URLs that begin with "https" indicate that an SSL connection will be used.

Storefront: A prefabricated set of Web pages containing information about a business or company.

Super Affiliates: The top 1 or 2 percent of affiliates that generate approximately 90 percent of any affiliate program's earnings.

T

Tagging: A method applied to blog posts and social bookmarking pages to make them more accessible both to the user and the search engine spiders.

Targeted Marketing: The process of distinguishing the different groups that make up a market and developing appropriate products and marketing mixes for each targeted market involved.

Text Link: A link not accompanied by a graphic image.

Third-Party Credit Card Processor: A company that accepts credit card orders on behalf of another company, making a merchant account unnecessary.

Third-Party Tracking Software: Software located on a server other than the user's that tracks and records visits to a Web site.

Tracking Method: The method by which an affiliate program tracks referred sales, leads, or clicks.

Tracking URL: A Web site URL such as http://www.awebsite.com, with your special code attached to it, for example, http://www.awebsite.com/?myID. Visitors arriving at the site are tracked back to you through your special code, or ID.

Two Tier: Affiliate program structure in which affiliates earn commissions on their conversions as well as the conversions of webmasters they refer to the program.

U

Uniform Resource Locator (URL):   The address of a site on the World Wide Web. Here's an example URL: http://netprofitstoday.com/software/index.html. The "http" stands for "hypertext transfer protocol"; "://" signals the beginning of the address; "netprofitstoday.com" is the domain name; "software" is the directory or folder name; and "index.html" is the name of the HTML file.

Unique User: A visitor to a Web site; probably the best indicator of site traffic.

Upload: Transfer of a file from one computer to another computer.

User Session: The session of activity for one user on a Web site.

V

Viral Marketing: Describes any strategy that encourages individuals to pass on a marketing message to others, creating the potential for exponential growth in the message's exposure and influence. Like viruses, such strategies take advantage of rapid multiplication to explode the message to thousands and even millions.

Virtual Reality Markup Language (VRML):   A language developed as a replacement for HTML. At a VRML Web site, one can explore environments in three dimensions and interact with other people who are visiting the same site. VRML requires a special browser.

Virus: A set of commands, created intentionally, that will do some level of damage to a computer. A computer virus does not float around in cyberspace, but is always attached to something. That something could be a text file (MSWord document), an e-mail, a photo, a music clip, or a video clip. Your computer must receive one of these carriers in order to get a computer virus.

VoIP (Voice over Internet Protocol):   The technology used to transmit voice conversations over a data network using the Internet Protocol. Such a data network may be the Internet or a corporate Intranet.

W

Warez: Refers primarily to copyrighted material traded in violation of copyright law. The term generally refers to illegal releases by organized groups, as opposed to peer-to-peer file sharing between friends or large groups of people with a similar interest.

Webmaster: The person at your Internet service provider who is responsible for maintaining the server. Also, any person who maintains a Web site.

Web Site: A collection of HTML pages.

Wide Area Network (WAN):   Large computers linked together over a long distance via phone or wireless communication.

World Wide Web (WWW or Web):   A section of the Internet containing "pages" of information, including text, photos, graphics, audio, and video. You can search for documents by using one of the many search databases. To access the Web, you must use a browser.

Y

Yahoo!:   The most popular and (perhaps) the most comprehensive of all search index databases on the World Wide Web. Yahoo's URL is http:// www.yahoo.com.

Appendix A
Most Popular Affiliate Networks

CLICKBANK

ClickBank (http://clickbank.com) distributes over 10,000 digital products and services through a network of over 100,000 affiliates, and the checks arrive like clockwork. ClickBank withholds 10 percent from each check to cover its risk of future returns. The holdbacks are credited to your account after about 90 days. You do not have to wait for acceptance from individual merchants. Simply browse the marketplace, get and post your link, and start making money.

COMMISSION JUNCTION

Commission Junction (http://cj.com) refers to its affiliates as publishers and its merchants as advertisers. There are no sign-up restrictions other than nonacceptance of sites that contain the following or provide links to sites that contain any of the following: libelous, defamatory, obscene, abusive, violent, bigoted, hate-oriented, illegal, cracking, hacking or warez content or offers of any illegal goods or services. Turnaround time on the application is very quick.

LINKSHARE

Linkshare (http://linkshare.com) reports over 10 million partnerships in the network and claims to be the most successful pay-for-performance (affiliate) network of its kind. Linkshare sends commission payment for some merchants, while others process their own payments—sometimes in their own good time.

PERFORMICS

One of the bigger affiliate networks, Performics (http://Performics.com) had over 180 merchant partners at the time of this writing, including ADT, AOL, Bose, BlockBuster Online, Cabela's, Indigo Books & Music, Linens 'n Things, Magellan's, Motorola, Safeway, and the Body Shop.

SHAREASALE

ShareaSale (http://shareasale.com) has a couple of thousand merchant and product offers. Clients include Avitan Technologies Corp., Glamor Shades, DanceSavvy, World Speakers Association, Student Planner, and Bonsai Boy of New York.

Appendix B
Additional
Affiliate Networks

- AdReporting.com
- AffiliateBot.com
- AffiliateCop.com
- AffiliateCrew.com
- AffiliateFuel.com
- AffiliateFuture.co.uk
- AffiliateNetwork.com
- AffiliateWindow.com
- BidClix.com
- CasinoCoins.com
- CasinoRewards.com
- ClickxChange.com
- ClixGalore.com
- CommissionSoup.com
- CPAEmpireAffiliate.com
- CyberBounty.com

- DarkBlue.com
- eAdvertising.com
- FineClicks.com
- iCommissions.com
- IncomeAccess.com
- iWhiz.com
- Kolimbo.com
- LeadHound.com
- MaxBounty.com
- OfferFusion.com
- OffersQuest.com
- PaidonResults.com
- PartnerWeekly.com
- PrimaryAds.com
- Quinstreet.com
- ReferBack.com
- Reporting.net
- RevenuePilot.com
- Search4Clicks.com
- SellShareware.com
- ShareResults.com
- TrafficDoubler.com

Appendix C
Recommended
Resources

TRADE PUBLICATIONS

- *Revenue Magazine* (http://www.RevenueToday.com). Published bimonthly, *Revenue* is the only magazine dedicated to the art of affiliate marketing.

BECOME A BETTER WRITER

If you have no writing experience or you want to brush up on your skills, here are books and tools that have helped me along the way. Read as much as you can on the subject, because the better you convey yourself in writing, the better your conversion rates will be.

- *Turn Words into Traffic* (http://www.NetProfitsToday.com/_resources/turn-words-into-traffic.html). Written by Jim and Dallas Edwards. Using the simple *"turn words into traffic"* system, your articles will soon be all over the Internet attracting visitors to your Website like bees to honey—even if you think you can't write.

- *Net Writing Masters Course* (http://netwriting.sitesell.
  com). Produced by Ken Evoy, the Net Writing Masters
  Course is a *free* e-mail course. Read it to become an effective
  "e-persuader."

- *Make Your Content Pre-Sell* (http://mycps.sitesell.com). Do
  you think that you are not a writer? Well, you are, and Ken
  Evoy will prove it to you.

- *Ultimate Copywriting Workshop* (http://ultimatecopywriting
  workshop.com). Yanik Silver describes the ability to put
  words on a computer screen and have people send you money
  as "the ultimate security in a very un-secure world....Your
  ability to produce cash on demand through the power of
  your pen or keyboard is truly the equivalent of modern day
  alchemy." Visit the site to get access to a free 143-page
  PDF file and 1-hour audio presentation on the subject of
  copywriting.

SOURCES OF PREWRITTEN CONTENT

- *PLR Information* (http://www.netprofitstoday.com/_
  resources/private-label-rights.html). You will find information about private label rights along with a number of PLR
  distributors.

- *Public Domain Riches* (http://www.publicdomainriches.
  com). Learn how to source public domain works to sell as
  your own material.

SOFTWARE SUGGESTION

- *Headline Creator Pro Software* (http://ezheadlines.
  com). Headlines are what your visitors see first. It does

not matter how well-written your copy is; if your headlines do not grab your visitors attention, your message will not get read. Developed by Scott Britner, this software is based on the best headlines ever written and actually writes headlines for you.

Index

A

MSN.com, 151
Multilevel marketing (MLM),
  120, 124, 127
My Yahoo!, 161
MyAffiliateProgram, 145
MySimon.com, 70

N

Natural search engine results,
  53–54
Navigation, 76
Net Writing Masters Course, 234
NetMechanic, 191
NetProfitsToday Forum, 156
Netscape Communicator/
  Navigator, 111
Network marketing, 127
Newsletter, 87, 144, 199
Nextag.com, 60
Niche, 23, 65–66. *See also* Market
  research
Nike, 75
NotePad, 9–10

O

ODP, 170
Offline marketing strategies,
  164–168
One-time expenses, 11
101Date.com, 73, 75
Online Directory Project (ODP), 170
Online Publishers Association, 36
Optional purchases, 12–13

Organic search engine results,
  53–55
Organize your affiliate data, 4–5
OrganizedAffiliate.com, 7

P

Paint Shop Pro, 102
PartnerIndustry.com, 44
Partnership and percentage partners
  programs, 124
Pay-per-click (PPC) advertising,
  55, 140–142
Pay-per-click (PPC) programs, 124
Pay-per-lead programs, 124
Pay-per-sale programs, 124
Payment schedules, 130
PayPal.com, 130
PayPerClickSearchEngines.com, 142
Performance data. *See* Adding it
  all up
Performics.com, 42, 230
Pirillo, Chris, 137
Pitfalls, 197–209
  application rejected, 201, 202
  application terminated, 202–207
  commission theft, 207
  content theft, 207–208
  mistakes to avoid, 197–201
  unfair PPC competitors, 208
PLR articles, 90, 92
PLR Information, 234
Plus sign, 43
Pop-ups, 110, 199

About the Author

Rosalind Gardner is recognized worldwide as a leading authority on the topic of affiliate marketing. As a speaker, author, and consultant, Rosalind teaches her students how to create online businesses without having products of their own. She also teaches merchants how to use affiliate marketing to promote their products online—for free. With her help, many of her clients are now earning hefty six-figure incomes.

In late 1997, Rosalind was working as an air traffic controller in Canada and didn't have a shred of business experience that might have helped her escape the ATC shift schedules or the frozen north. However, a single click on a banner ad that read, "Webmasters Make Money" changed her life completely for the better. *Much* better.

Rosalind received her first affiliate commission check a month later, and by the end of her first year as an affiliate marketer she was netting $5,000 per month. In early 2000, she traded her career as an air traffic controller for full-time *netpreneurship,* and in 2002 Rosalind earned over $436,797 in commissions selling other people's stuff online. She now earns much more than that selling everything from dating services to watches to webmaster tools, and she helps other people do the same.

Rosalind's various Internet publishing projects entertain and inform millions of visitors annually while earning her a high six-figure personal income. When asked what she enjoys most about making a living online from home, her answer was, "Having the freedom to do what I want, when I want!"

Rosalind is the author of the best-selling *Super Affiliate Handbook: How I Made $436,797 in One Year Selling Other People's Stuff Online,* and she writes the "Affiliate's Corner" column for *Revenue Magazine—The Performance Marketing Standard,* the only glossy magazine representing the affiliate marketing industry.

She coproduced "The Affiliate Business Blueprint" (Affiliate BusinessBlueprint.com), a multimedia product including audio files and transcripts, with Jim Edwards, and in 2006 she opened the Blog Classroom (BlogClassroom.com) with Anik Singal, CEO of Affiliate Classroom.

Rosalind lives in the beautiful Okanagan Valley of British Columbia, Canada. Her online business affords her a healthy and active lifestyle that includes running, yoga, and only the finest of beers.